STANISLAV GROF
LSD PIONEER

"Stan Grof may have contributed as much to our understanding of the human mind, its potentials, pathologies, and possibilities, as Freud or Jung or Maslow. We will be exploring the far-reaching implications of his many discoveries—so beautifully described and acknowledged in this book—for decades."

ROGER WALSH, M.D., PH.D., PROFESSOR AT THE
UNIVERSITY OF CALIFORNIA, IRVINE

"Stan is the primary catalyst of the psychedelic renaissance. He kept the psychedelic flame alive in the dark decades of the global suppression of psychedelic research. This book is a gift of love from Brigitte to Stan and from Brigitte to the world."

RICK DOBLIN, PH.D., FOUNDER AND PRESIDENT OF THE
MULTIDISCIPLINARY ASSOCIATION FOR PSYCHEDELIC STUDIES (MAPS)

"Stan, you are a light and inspiration to me and many others. Your far-sighted and prophetic work is helping to transform our culture for the better."

RUPERT SHELDRAKE, PH.D., AUTHOR OF
WAYS TO GO BEYOND AND WHY THEY WORK

"Brigitte's creative homage to Stan is a book of treasures for all those who have been influenced and inspired by this extraordinary thinker, visionary, and healer: the wonderful personal photos, the history and memories, the loving tributes from friends and colleagues, and the long interview, in which he shares his newly clarified understanding of the human psyche, revising his cartography to reflect his recognition of the superordinate role of the archetypes as they inform the perinatal matrices, the COEX systems, and the transpersonal."

RICHARD TARNAS, PROFESSOR OF PHILOSOPHY, COSMOLOGY, AND
CONSCIOUSNESS AT THE CALIFORNIA INSTITUTE OF INTEGRAL STUDIES

"There are few people in the world today who have made a truly fundamental discovery not only about the world but also about us and our real selves. Stan Grof is one of these people. His thoughts and work will live many times more than him to benefit our understanding of life, mind, and that deep layer that we call psyche."

ERVIN LASZLO, PH.D., PHILOSOPHER OF
SCIENCE AND SYSTEMS THEORIST

"Stan changed the course of psychedelic history and touched the lives of a generation. The pictures included alone are a treasure, and the tributes give glimpses into the psychedelic community that has surrounded him."

CHRISTOPHER M. BACHE, PH.D., AUTHOR OF
LSD AND THE MIND OF THE UNIVERSE

STANISLAV GROF
LSD PIONEER

FROM PHARMACOLOGY
TO ARCHETYPES

BRIGITTE GROF

Park Street Press
Rochester, Vermont

Park Street Press
One Park Street
Rochester, Vermont 05767
www.ParkStPress.com

Park Street Press is a division of Inner Traditions International

Originally published in 2021 in German under the title *Stanislav Grof und das LSD: Von der Pharmakologie zu den Archetypen; Eine Hommage zum 90. Geburtstag* by Nachtschatten Verlag
Published in 2021 in French under the title *Stanislav Grof et le LSD: De la pharmacologie aux archétypes; Un livre Hommage pour ses 90 ans* by Les éditions Transpersonnelles
First U.S. edition published in 2023 by Park Street Press; this translation published by exclusive license from Nachtschatten Verlag and the agency of Agence Schweiger

Cataloging-in-Publication Data for this title is available from the Library of Congress

ISBN 978-1-64411-946-4 (print)
ISBN 978-1-64411-947-1 (ebook)

Printed and bound in China by Reliance Printing Co., Ltd.

10 9 8 7 6 5 4 3 2 1

Original text design and layout by Nina Seiler and Silvia Aeschbach; additional U.S. edition typesetting by Virginia Scott Bowman
This book was typeset in Adobe Caslon

To send correspondence to the author of this book, mail a first-class letter to the author c/o Inner Traditions • Bear & Company, One Park Street, Rochester, VT 05767, and we will forward the communication, or contact the author directly at **BrigitteGrof.com**.

Contents

Stan Grof in Big Sur 2017

DEDICATION

To Stan,
for the celebration of your 90th birthday.

With deep gratitude and much love for your lifelong research into the healing power of psychedelics, holotropic breathwork, Transpersonal Psychology, and holotropic states of consciousness. Your loving, compassionate, selfless, and humble service to humanity has helped to bring back into the world the spiritual knowledge of who we really are.

You are not only an incredible researcher, scientist, scholar, psychiatrist, and psychotherapist, with such vast knowledge and experience. You are also a wonderful human being with the biggest loving heart I have ever met, such beautiful eyes, wild sense of humor and unlimited curiosity, compassionate and free spirit, gentle and strong at the same time.

You are the love of my lives, the other half of my soul. Having traveled many inner and outer journeys together, I feel blessed by the gift of our unconditional love and I am honored and endlessly grateful to be your wife.

I am also speaking for the many people around the world whose lives, hearts, and souls you have deeply touched and transformed through your work and your being.

We wish you a very Happy Birthday!

May you be happy, healthy, and well for many more years and have many interesting adventures to come.

With all my heart,
Your Brigitte

Stan and Brigitte Grof in Esalen 2017

Birthday Greetings

Dearest Stan,

Our lives have now been closely linked for over eight decades.

It would be hard to choose an event that reflects this tie most.

You have had such a profound impact on my life, both in practical terms and conceptually. From the practical point, arguably the most important has been you inviting me to visit you in America. The visit was planned for two months. Fifty-three years later I'm still on this side of the Atlantic. Quite a visit!

You have also had a profound impact on all my thinking. And after studying neurobiology of non-ordinary mood states of consciousness, their unfolding during lifetime, and their manifestations in large families, all my observations indicate that these experiences cannot be generated by the brain. They appear to be emerging from the field of consciousness.

A realization that you reached already during your first LSD-25 self-experiment sixty-five years ago, and for which I was a sitter.

Much love, and many more years, which we all again plan to share with you.

Paul Grof, M.D., Ph.D., psychiatrist,
professor for mood disorders, Toronto

Ottawa, 30 March 2021

Paul and Stan Grof in China 2015

My dear heart friend Stan,

Age 90 is majestic and also limited . . .

to me, you are an immortal being.

In your ninety circles of seasons around our star you have been for me an inspiration and colleague, a visionary companion and extraordinary teacher and playmate.

In each incarnation we may be fortunate to meet a few truly remarkable people whose genius and vision and heart change the course of our lives.

You have been that for me. The breadth of your understanding, the new and profound maps and practices you have discovered or rediscovered, the cosmic perspective you offered me and all those in your orbit have been powerful forces for learning and awakening and bringing more compassion into our lives.

I could go on about the multiple dimensions of your knowledge and understanding, from psychology and psychiatry to modern physics, world music, art, literature, languages, anthropology and mythology, systems theory astronomy, astrology and all forms of human transformation.

But these, magnificent dimensions they are, creative aspects of your mind and vision are embedded in something more important.

This is your wise, preternaturally steady, hugely compassionate and boundlessly interested spirit . . . which meets the unbearable beauty and ocean of tears that make up our human incarnation and the cosmos beyond . . . in a loving, caring, curious, and liberated way.

Jack Kornfield and Stan Grof in China 2015

You are the master of the cosmic game, and it has been a blessing and an honor to share nearly half a century of loving connection, creative collaboration, and inspiration.

Just as Albert Hofmann enjoyed his last decade with pleasure and a magical triumph, may this 90th year be the beginning of a special nourishing decade full of yet more adventures and love.

Blessings to you and the most wonderful Brigitte with you,

Jack Kornfield, Buddhist Vipassana teacher and author

To my beloved friend on his 90th solar return

There is no one in my life quite comparable to you, dear Stan, in the many profound ways you have influenced me, not only in the unfolding of my mind but of my soul and spirit. You and I have both been blessed by many brilliant teachers and thinkers, but for me you are in a class by yourself. What an amazing gift of grace you have been.

Looking back now over almost half a century since we both arrived at Esalen, I carry in my mind's eye the hundreds of lecture halls and classrooms and stages where we have lectured together, in so many countries across the world's continents, starting in Esalen's Big House living room and Huxley and on to Prague and Zürich, to Hollyhock and Eranos, to Brazil and China. We have faced situations that were dangerous and enjoyed others that were idyllic. We have grappled together with complex ideas and felt the joy of astonishing discoveries. I barely ever have a deep thought that has not in some fundamental way been shaped by your insights and your influence.

And through it all, I cannot remember a single time when there was not the feeling of affectionate friendship and gladness in your company. The warm light of your smiling eyes radiates from a great depth of spirit that all of us recognize in you. (Just ask your loving soulmate, Brigitte.) While surely many gods and goddesses express themselves through all of us, I sometimes have had the feeling that in your gentle masculine form this lifetime the Great Mother Goddess has shone through with special power. How many thousands of people you have cared for, brought to a new birth, with such skill, kindness, patience, and wisdom. You have been a midwife of the soul for so many. But more than this, through your courage, your calm equilibrium, your trust in the universe and the unique healing intelligence deep within every person, you have in a very real way been the vessel of the Great Mother's boundless love so that others can carry that gift within themselves. How else to explain that it was in your presence that so many have experienced birth and rebirth, the unmistakable sign that a mother goddess is present?

You came into a modern world where the ancient mysteries and sacred rituals were lost to our civilization. Throughout the many decades of your life you have been a high priest of the death-rebirth mystery religions from millennia ago, a shaman from the great indigenous traditions, somehow transported into the world of science and psychiatry. And somehow through your amazing strength and capaciousness, and no doubt through karma and grace, you have managed to hold that

Rick Tarnas and Stan Grof, Esalen 1985

great tension of opposites and bring them together into a true synthesis, a sacred marriage that will continue to bear fruit for generations to come.

These words gesture toward your special historical role, but above all here I just want to thank you for the immense gift of your personal presence. So kind you have been, so generous, helping to guide my inner journey from those earliest years. And you have served for me as a model for how to stand before the world and speak of realities that deeply challenge the conventional mindset and offer new paths of wisdom and healing.

All honor to you, Stan, and my unending gratitude. May your star continue shining brightly, through this lifetime and many to come.

Rick Tarnas,
professor of philosophy, cosmology, and consciousness,
California Institute of Integral Studies

Rick Doblin and Stan Grof, Mill Valley 2018

As you turn 90, it's my birthday wish that you see with your own eyes the first FDA approval of psychedelic-assisted therapy, probably MDMA-assisted therapy for PTSD, and then psilocybin for depression and then others. It will be the fruit of the tree that you planted from being present at the beginnings of LSD research, participating in outstanding LSD research teams in Prague and at Spring Grove, experiencing the backlash, writing foundational books about LSD research, starting holotropic breathwork, and helping build Transpersonal Psychology and the International Transpersonal Association, and over the ensuing decades training many of today's leading psychedelic therapists/researchers.

Albert and Anita lived long enough to see the beginning of the resumption of LSD research after decades of repression, in one of my prouder achievements at MAPS. My 90th birthday wish for you is health to experience in your own lifetime the fruition of legal psychedelic-assisted therapy by prescription covered by health insurance, your legacy.

Rick Doblin, Ph.D., executive director and founder of MAPS
(Multidisciplinary Association for Psychedelic Studies)

In Celebration of Stan's 90th Birthday

How do I begin to express the memories of 50+ years and capture them with a few words? It is not possible. To say that it has been a full-on adventure is a start. We (Michael and I) have been witness to and shared extraordinary events with you. Some were mundane and some were truly special; all were creative, generous, and humorous. Your special gift of serious intent and determination combined simultaneously with that twinkle in your eyes is unforgettable.

Thanks to you. True friendship lives in all who have the privilege of knowing you.

With love and gratitude,
Sandra Harner, Ph.D., cofounder and vice president
of the Foundation of Shamanic Studies

Sandy and Michael Harner, Stan Grof, Mill Valley 2016

Dear Stan

What a gift it has been to know you over these last forty years!

You have been so many things to me and to so many others:
- a dear friend,
- trailblazer,
- Way shower,
- door opener,
- map maker,
- conference creator,
- inspiration,
- growth catalyst,
- life changer,
- and consciousness expander

It's a long list!

You've done and created so much:
1. you've deepened and spiritualized psychology,
2. created transpersonal psychology,
3. mapped consciousness across cultures and disciplines,
4. integrated psychologies, mythology, and spirituality,
5. discovered new practices such as holotropic breathwork,
6. recognized new spiritual challenges such as spiritual emergence and spiritual emergency,
7. founded new organizations such as the International Transpersonal Association and the Spiritual Emergence Network, and
8. applied these insights to understanding our individual, social, and global problems.

Again, it's a long list.

Yet as Ken Wilber once said to me, "If Stan had only written *The Cosmic Game,* he'd still deserve a place in history."

It will probably take decades for the full significance and many implications of your work to be fully understood and appreciated.

Roger Walsh, Michael Harner and Stan Grof, California 2016

But no matter when that may be, you have clearly expanded and deepened our understanding of human nature—of human psychology, potentials, possibilities, pathologies, and therapies—as very few in history have done. To the extent that your discoveries are recognized and implemented, to that extent the world will be a better place, with less personal pain and collective suffering, and greater flourishing and well-being.

It's now been nine decades, 90 years, that you have explored and delighted in life. You have explored, discovered, lived, and loved so much, thanks to your prodigious intellect, huge heart, joyful curiosity, and fearless willingness to transcend conventions and barbecue sacred cows.

Stan, you are a priceless gift to us all, and perhaps in time you will be recognized as a world treasure. You are truly a Master of the Cosmic Game.

Thank you, dear friend, for all you have given to me and to the world, and were Frances here, she would want to thank you just as much as I do.

With gratitude and love,
Roger Walsh, M.D., Ph.D., professor for psychiatry, philosophy,
and anthropology at University of California, Irvine

Dear Stan,

On the occasion of your 90th birthday, I want to celebrate your long life and express gratitude for Ralph and myself that our paths crossed with yours so deeply in this lifetime. Indeed it was a fortuitous meeting when you made that unexpected stop with Peter John at Millbrook in 1965 and met Ralph. You remained good friends for over fifty years, and we have been fortunate enough to live in the same area and meet at various social occasions.

I feel fortunate to have been included by you and your circle of friendship through Ralph. I honor that you had a close friendship with Ralph's beloved partner Angeles Arrien. I was grateful that though I was so much younger, you embraced me as Ralph's new partner.

I call in a special evening that you and Christina and Ralph and I had in May 2014 at the Taj Restaurant in San Rafael after Angie died April 24, 2014, and before Christina's death June 15, 2014. We marked that evening with the affirmation of friendship, between the thin veils of life and death of two wonderful and important women in yours and Ralph's life.

I am full of gratitude for the way that you and Brigitte embraced Ralph and me in your wonderful new love relationship, and I celebrate the invigorating life you and Brigitte have created together that nourishes all of us.

As you celebrate your nine decades in this lifetime, I salute your great life as an academic, explorer, writer, teacher, leader of holotropic breathwork, and as a sweet friend. I was so fortunate that my first holotropic breathwork experience was at IONS under your leadership, and that I got lucky that you were the facilitator for the small processing group that I was in. I am also grateful to you for your support of my vision to create ITA Youth Conferences, a passion and mission of mine to empower young people through expansive experiences. The ITA conferences were awesome and unforgettable for us and for all who attended

Our lives traverse academic, intellectual content about transpersonal psychological and psychedelic subjects, astrological knowledge and interests, awesome conference gatherings, and intimate, playful social gatherings with dear friends.

Here is the toast that I think Ralph was giving in the picture above that Brigitte took at Betsy Gordon's home, I think in celebration of your marriage to Brigitte.

Cathy Coleman, Ph.D., astrologer

Ralph Metzner and his wife Cathy Coleman, California 2016

The L's Toast by Ralph Metzner

The 4 L's (Elves)	The 8 L's (Elves)
Life	*Langes Leben*
Love	*Light of Love*
Laughter	*Lusty Laughter*
Letting Be	*Lightly Letting Be*

Stan and Brigitte Grof, Brother David Steindl-Rast, ITA Coference, Prague 2017

This picture, dear Stan, shows you at your jovial best, your face lit up by the radiance shining from Brigitte's eyes. It captures a moment I treasure and reminds me of so many blessed moments I was privileged to share with you. What a great gift our friendship has been for me these decades!

Your 90th birthday is an occasion to thank you for this gift. It also reminds me what a privilege it was to meet your mother. How grateful I am to have met that great lady who gave you to us 90 years ago. Don't let that number 90 frighten you. Being half a decade ahead of you in counting birthdays, I can reassure you: in spite of the inevitable limitations, the 90s can be a time of growing sweetness. And with Brigitte at your side, how could this not be so?

Thus, I confidently wish you (with a poetic image borrowed from Rilke) that autumnal sunshine that drives the ultimate sweetness into the heavy wine of your life's accomplishments. God bless you on this special birthday and always.

With a festive hug,
Your Brother David (Benedictine monk and author)

Happy Birthday, Stan—your 90th!

We have known each other for fifty-seven years, sharing countless adventures and good works. For half a century now, we've traveled back and forth to Russia, weaving ties that help bring that stupendous nation to more fruitful relations with the West. Living at Esalen from 1972 until 1986 you did as much as anyone in the world to assemble leading thinkers in many fields for ventures that have been catalytic for consciousness research ever since. And along the way you have been a friend for the ages, guiding Dulce and me through interior journeys, helping shape some of our most fruitful endeavors, and providing perspectives that no one else can. You've been a blessing for us and countless others, Stan. Your life and work will resonate in the world at large for a long time to come.

With admiration, love, and gratitude,
Michael Murphy, author and cofounder of Esalen Institute

There are few people in the world today who have made a truly fundamental discovery not only about the world, but about us. About our real self. Stan Grof is one of these people. It is a privilege to know him and to share the vision he is bringing to life—about life, about the deepest sense and meaning of what it is to be alive.

His thought and work will live many times more than his ninety years. To benefit our understanding of life, mind, and that deep layer that we call psyche. Long life to Psychonaut Stanislav Grof!

Ervin Laszlo, Ph.D., philosopher of science, systems theorist

Brigitte and Stan Grof, Ervin Laszlo and Maria Sagi, ITA Coference, Prague 2017

Stan Grof and Fritjof Capra at Esalen 1977

My warmest wishes at your 90th for health, happiness, and serenity!

With gratitude for many decades of inspiring friendship,
Fritjof Capra, Ph.D., physicist and author

Rupert Sheldrake and Jill Purce

Happy Birthday, Stan! You are a light and inspiration to me, as you are to many others. Your farsighted and prophetic work is helping to transform our culture for the better, and I am sure it will continue to do so.

Rupert Sheldrake, Ph.D.,
author of Ways to Go Beyond and Why They Work

Dear Stan!

Your work and life have profoundly touched so many other people's lives. We're grateful to count our lives among them. Your writing inspired us and pointed us toward a compelling path at a time when we were looking for new directions. Over the ensuing thirty years, that path has taken us on our own "adventures of self-discovery," healing, and growth, as well as leading us into deeply rewarding and satisfying work with other people, including clinical research picking up a thread that you and others started long ago. It was your written work that pointed a direction for us, and it was your teaching and personal example in the Grof Training that showed us how the path could be followed skillfully and with heart. Over many hours, we had the opportunity to see your powerful framework for understanding the cartography of the psyche and the nature of the "inner healing intelligence" brought to life with your commitment and capacity to support individuals in their healing process. Working with people in long and intense holotropic breathwork sessions, you demonstrated again and again the power of compassionate presence and trust in the healing capacity of each individual and in the healing potential of non-ordinary states of consciousness. As psychedelics gain prominence in this culture again, this loving commitment and human connection is, for us, the heart of your amazing legacy.

Happy birthday and much love,
Annie Mithoefer, B.S.N., and Michael Mithoefer, M.D.,
world leaders in MDMA-assisted therapy

At the turn of the nineteenth and twentieth centuries, the Czech lands can be considered the cradle of critical thinking and music of late Romanticism. The roots of such greats as Antonín Dvořák, Leoš Janáček, Karl Popper, Kurt Gödel, Erich Korngold, and Franz Kafka go back to a relatively small area of Bohemia and Moravia in Central Europe. In the second half of the twentieth century, this region enriched world culture, philosophy, science, and sports with cosmopolitan figures who, thanks to their talent and greatness, achieved worldwide significance. In sports it was, for example, Martina Navrátilová, Ivan Lendl, or Jaromír Jágr, in film undoubtedly Miloš Forman, in literature Milan Kundera and in psychological sciences Stan Grof.

Several important historical circumstances came together in the case of Stan Grof. First, it is the "golden age" of the 1960s, when several enthusiasts began experimenting with hallucinogens and their application in psychotherapy at the Psychiatric Research Institute in Prague. The second important circumstance is a particular reflection of the relative limitations of reductionism in science and an understanding of our being's transcendental dimension. Stan Grof later elaborated on this area in his book *Beyond the Brain*.

And the third and perhaps most important circumstance in the case of Stan Grof was his emigration to the United States, which was forced by the invasion of Soviet troops into then Czechoslovakia. Hand in hand with the following era, during which psychedelics fell into disrepute due to restrictive substance abuse policy, Stan Grof extended his concept of LSD-induced altered state of consciousness not only to altered states of consciousness in general but also to transpersonal psychology.

With this overlap into the end of the twentieth century's philosophy and thought framework, Stan Grof became one of the above-mentioned cosmopolitan greats, whose roots lead to the same place. All future generations of scientists, thinkers, philosophers, and those interested in psychology will have to deal with Stan's work.

Stan Grof and Cyril Höschl, Prague

Whether it is an understanding or critical analysis, it will in any case be a lasting trace left by Stan Grof in human civilization, continuing the tradition of such greats as Sigmund Freud and Carl Gustav Jung. Grof's significant life anniversary is an excellent opportunity to sufficiently understand and appreciate the significance of his life's work.

Prof. MUDr. Cyril Höschl, DrSc., FRCPsych.,
director of the National Institute of Mental Health and
professor of psychiatry, Charles University, Prague

Albert Hofmann and Stan Grof at his home in Switzerland 1985

Foreword to Albert Hofmann's
LSD: My Problem Child by Stanislav Grof*

The use of psychedelic substances can be traced back for millennia, to the dawn of human history. Since time immemorial, plant materials containing powerful consciousness-expanding compounds have been used in many different parts of the world to induce non-ordinary states of consciousness in various ritual and spiritual contexts. They have played an important role in shamanic practice, aboriginal healing ceremonies, rites of passage, mysteries of death and rebirth, and spiritual traditions. The ancient and native cultures using psychedelic materials held them in great esteem and considered them to be sacraments, "flesh of the gods."

Human groups, which had at their disposal psychedelic plants, took advantage of their entheogenic effects (entheogenic means literally "awakening the divine within") and made them the principal vehicle of their ritual and spiritual life. The preparations made from these plants mediated for these people experiential contact with the archetypal dimensions of reality—deities, mythological realms, power animals, and numinous forces and aspects of nature. Another important area where states induced by psychedelics played a crucial role was diagnosing and healing of various disorders.

Anthropological literature contains many reports indicating that native cultures use psychedelics to cultivate intuition and extrasensory perception for a variety of divinatory, as well as practical purposes, such as finding lost persons and objects, obtaining information about people in remote locations, and for following the movement of the game these people hunted. In addition, psychedelic experiences served as important sources of artistic inspiration, providing ideas for rituals, paintings, sculptures, and songs.

In the history of Chinese medicine, reports about psychedelic substances can be traced back about 3,000 years. The legendary divine potion referred to as haoma in the ancient Persian Zend Avesta and as soma in the Indian Vedas was used by the Indo-Iranian tribes millenia ago. The mystical states of consciousness induced by soma were very likely the principal source of the Vedic and Hindu

* From *LSD: My Problem Child*, MAPS Edition 2005/2009

Mushroom Stone, ca. 1000 BC – 500 AD, Guatemala City. Photo from *The Wonderous Mushroom*, © Gordon Wasson

religion. Preparations from different varieties of hemp have been smoked and ingested under various names—*hashish, charas, bhang, ganja, kif,* and *marijuana*—in Asia, in Africa, and in the Caribbean area for recreation, pleasure, and during religious ceremonies. They represented an important sacrament for such diverse groups as the Indian Brahmans, certain orders of Sufis, ancient Scythians, and the Jamaican Rastafarians. Ceremonial use of various psychedelic substances also has a long history in Central America.

Highly effective mind-altering plants were well known in several Pre-Columbian Indian cultures—among the Aztecs, Mayans, Olmecs, and Mazatecs. The most famous of these are the Mexican cactus peyote (*Anhalonium lewinii*), the sacred mushroom teonanacatl (*Psilocybe mexicana*) and ololiuhqui, or morning glory seeds (*Rivea corymbosa*). These materials have been used as sacraments until this day by several Mexican Indian tribes (Huichols, Mazatecs, Cora people, and others) and by the Native American Church.

The famous South American *yajé* or *ayahuasca* is a decoction from a jungle liana (*Banisteriopsis caapi*) with other plant additives. The Amazonian area is also known for a variety of psychedelic snuffs (*Virola calophylla, Piptadenia peregrina*). Preparations from the bark of the shrub iboga (*Tabernanthe iboga*) have been used by African tribes in lower dosage as a stimulant during lion hunts and long canoe trips and in higher doses as a ritual sacrament. The above list represents only a small fraction of psychedelic compounds that have been used over many centuries in various countries of the world. The impact that the experiences encountered in these states had on the spiritual and cultural life of pre-industrial societies has been enormous.

People from our culture, who see the use of psychedelic plants as something that is practiced in exotic and "primitive" cultures and is alien to our own tradition would be very surprised to find out that psychedelic substances very likely profoundly influenced the ancient Greek culture, generally considered the cradle of the European civilization. Many giants of Greek culture, including Plato, Aristotle,

Huichol Yarn Painting

Alkibiades, Pindaros, and others were initiates in the Mediterranean mysteries of death and rebirth held in the names of Demeter and Persephone, Dionysus, Attis, Adonis, Orpheus, and others. According to a theory proposed by a research team that included Albert Hofmann himself, the sacred potion kykeon administered to thousands of initiates in the Eleusinian mysteries every five years for almost two millennia contained an ergot alkaloid similar to LSD. Psychedelics were also very likely ingredients in the wines used for the Bacchanalia.

The long history of ritual use of psychedelic plants contrasts sharply with a relatively short history of scientific efforts to identify their psychoactive alkaloids and to study their effects. The first psychedelic substance that was synthetized in a chemically pure form and systematically explored under laboratory conditions was

Model of the Telestrion, the Eleusinian sanctuary

mescaline, the active alkaloid from the peyote cactus. Clinical experiments conducted with this substance in the first three decades of the twentieth century focused on the phenomenology of the mescaline experience and its interesting effects on artistic perception and creative expression. Surprisingly, they did not reveal its therapeutic, heuristic, and entheogenic potential. Kurt Beringer, author of the influential book *Der Meskalinrausch* (Mescaline Inebriation) published in 1927, concluded that mescaline induced a toxic psychosis. After these pioneering clinical experiments with mescaline, very little research was done in this fascinating problem area until Albert Hofmann's 1942 epoch-making serendipitous discovery of the psychedelic properties of LSD-25, or diethylamid of lysergic acid, a substance of extraordinary potency. This new semisynthetic ergot derivative, active in incredibly minute quantities of micrograms or gammas (millionths of a gram), started a revolutionary era of research in psychopharmacology, psychology, psychiatry, and psychotherapy. Because of the incredible promises it held in many different fields of research, this new substance appeared to be Albert Hofmann's "prodigious child."

The discovery of powerful psychedelic effects of miniscule dosages of LSD started what has been called a "golden era of psychopharmacology." During a relatively short period of time, the joint efforts of biochemists, pharmacologists, neurophysiologists, psychiatrists, and psychologists succeeded in laying the foundations of a new scientific discipline that can be referred to as "pharmacology of consciousness." The active substances from several remaining psychedelic plants were chemically identified and prepared in chemically pure form. Following the discovery of

Albert Hofmann in his Basel laboratory at the time when he discovered LSD

the psychedelic effects of LSD-25, Albert Hofmann identified the active principles of the Mexican magic mushrooms (*Psilocybe mexicana*), psilocybin and psilocin, and that of ololiuhqui, or morning glory seeds (*Rivea corymbosa*), which turned out to be lysergic acid amide, closely related to LSD-25.

The armamentarium of psychedelic substances was further enriched by psychoactive derivatives of tryptamine—DMT (dimethyltryptamine), DET (diethyltryptamine), and DPT (dipropyltryptamine)—synthetized and studied by the Budapest group of chemists, headed by Steven Szara. The active principle from the African shrub *Tabernanthe iboga*, ibogaine, and the pure alkaloid from aya-huasca's main ingredient *Banisteriopsis caapi*, known under the names harmaline, yageine, and telepathine, had already been isolated and chemically identified earlier in the twentieth century. In the 1950s, a wide range of psychedelic alkaloids in pure form was available to researchers. It was now possible to study their properties in the laboratory and explore the phenomenology of their clinical effects and their therapeutic potential. The revolution triggered by Albert Hofmann's serendipitous discovery of LSD was underway.

After the publication of the first clinical paper on LSD by Walter A. Stoll in the late 1940s, in which the author described the effects of this extraordinary substance in a group of volunteers and psychiatric patients and mentioned its possible therapeutic potential, Albert Hofmann's "wonder child" became an overnight sensation in the scientific world. Never before in the history of science had a single substance held so much promise in such a wide variety of fields.

For neuropharmacologists and neurophysiologists, the discovery of LSD meant the beginning of a golden era of research that could solve many puzzles concerning neuroreceptors, synaptic transmitters, chemical antagonisms, the role of serotonin in the brain, and the intricate biochemical interactions underlying cerebral processes.

Experimental psychiatrists saw LSD as a unique means for creating a laboratory model for naturally occurring functional, or endogenous, psychoses. They hoped that the "experimental psychosis," induced by miniscule dosages of this substance, could provide unparalleled insights into the nature of these mysterious disorders and open new avenues for their treatment. It was suddenly conceivable that the brain or other parts of the body could under certain circumstances produce small quantities of a substance with similar effects as LSD. This meant that disorders like schizophrenia would not be mental diseases, but metabolic aberrations that could be counteracted by specific chemical intervention. The promise of this research was nothing less than the fulfillment of the dream of biologically oriented clinicians, the Holy Grail of psychiatry—a test-tube cure for schizophrenia.

LSD was also highly recommended as an extraordinary unconventional teaching device that would make it possible for clinical psychiatrists, psychologists, medical students, and nurses to spend a few hours in the world of their patients and as a result of it to understand them better, be able to communicate with them more effectively, and improve their ability to help them. Thousands of mental health professionals took advantage of this unique opportunity. These experiments brought surprising and astonishing results. They not only provided deep insights into the world of psychiatric patients, but also revolutionized the understanding of the nature and dimensions of the human psyche.

Many found that the current model, limiting the psyche to postnatal biography and the Freudian individual unconscious, was superficial and inadequate. The new map of the psyche that emerged out of this research added two large transbiographical domains—the perinatal level, closely related to the memory of biological birth, and the transpersonal level, harboring the historical and archetypal domains of the collective unconscious as envisioned by C. G. Jung. Early experiments with LSD showed that the roots of emotional and psychosomatic disorders were not limited to traumatic memories from childhood and infancy, as traditional psychiatrists assumed, but reached much deeper into the psyche, into the perinatal and transpersonal regions. Reports from psychedelic psychotherapists revealed LSD's unique potential as a powerful tool offering the possibility of deepening and accelerating the psychotherapeutic process.

Using LSD as a catalyst, it became possible to extend the range of applicability of psychotherapy to categories of patients that previously had been difficult to reach—sexual deviants, alcoholics, narcotic drug addicts, and criminal recidivists. Particularly valuable and promising were the early efforts to use LSD psychotherapy in the work with terminal cancer patients. Research on this population showed that LSD was able to relieve severe pain, often even in those patients who had not responded to medication with narcotics. In a large percentage of these patients, it was also possible to ease or even eliminate difficult emotional and psychosomatic symptoms, such as depression, general tension, and insomnia, alleviate the fear of death, increase the quality of their life during the remaining days, and positively transform the experience of dying.

For historians and critics of art, the LSD experiments provided extraordinary new insights into the psychology and psychopathology of art, particularly various modern movements, such as abstractionism, cubism, surrealism, fantastic realism, and into paintings and sculptures of various native, so-called primitive cultures. For professional painters, who participated in LSD research, the psychedelic session often marked a radical change in their artistic expression. Their imagination became much richer, their colors more vivid, and their style considerably freer. They could also often reach into deep recesses of their unconscious psyche and tap archetypal sources of inspiration. On occasion, people who had never painted before were able to produce extraordinary pieces of art.

LSD experimentation brought also fascinating observations, which were of great interest to spiritual teachers and scholars of comparative religion. The mystical experiences frequently observed in LSD sessions offered a radically new understanding of a wide variety of phenomena from the world of religion, including shamanism, the rites of passage, the ancient mysteries of death and rebirth, the

Universal Mother, painting by visionary artist Martina Hoffmann

Eastern spiritual philosophies, and the mystical traditions of the world. The fact that LSD and other psychedelic substances were able to trigger a broad range of spiritual experiences became the subject of heated scientific discussions. They revolved around the fascinating problem concerning the nature and value of this "instant" or "chemical" mysticism. LSD research seemed to be well on its way to fulfill all the above promises and expectations when it was suddenly interrupted by the unsupervised mass experimentation of the young generation. In the infamous Harvard affair, Timothy Leary, Richard Alpert, and Ralph Metzner left the university (Leary and Alpert leaving teaching posts, and Metzner losing a fellowship) after their overeager proselytizing of LSD and psilocybin. The ensuing repressive measures of administrative, legal, and political nature had very little effect on street

Ralph Metzner, Timothy Leary, and Richard Alpert (Ram Dass),1965

use of LSD and other psychedelics, but they drastically terminated legitimate clinical research. However, while the problems associated with this development were blown out of proportion by sensation-hunting journalists, this was not the only reason why LSD and other psychedelics were rejected by the Euro-American culture. An important contributing factor was also the attitude of technological societies toward non-ordinary states of consciousness.

As I mentioned earlier, all ancient and pre-industrial societies held these states in high esteem, whether they were induced by psychedelic plants or some of the many powerful non-drug "technologies of the sacred"—fasting, sleep deprivation, social and sensory isolation, dancing, chanting, music, drumming, or physical pain. Members of these social groups had the opportunity to repeatedly experience non-ordinary states of consciousness during their lives in a variety of sacred and secular contexts. By comparison, the industrial civilizations have pathologized non-ordinary states, developed effective means of suppressing them when they occur spontaneously, and have rejected or even outlawed the contexts and tools that can facilitate them. Because of the resulting naiveté and ignorance concerning non-ordinary states, Western culture was unprepared to accept and incorporate the extraordinary mind-altering properties and power of LSD and other psychedelics. The sudden invasion of the Dionysian element from the depths of the unconscious

THE

PSYCHEDELIC EXPERIENCE

A MANUAL BASED ON THE TIBETAN BOOK OF THE DEAD

BY
TIMOTHY LEARY, Ph.D.
RALPH METZNER, Ph.D.
RICHARD ALPERT, Ph.D.

The authors were engaged in a program of experiments
with LSD and other psychedelic drugs at Harvard University,
until sensational national publicity, unfairly concentrating
on student interest in the drugs, led to the suspension
of the experiments. Since then, the authors
have continued their work without
academic auspices

Timothy Leary, Ralph Metzner, and Richard Alpert
The Psychedelic Experience: A Manual Based on the Tibetan Book of the Dead, USA 1964

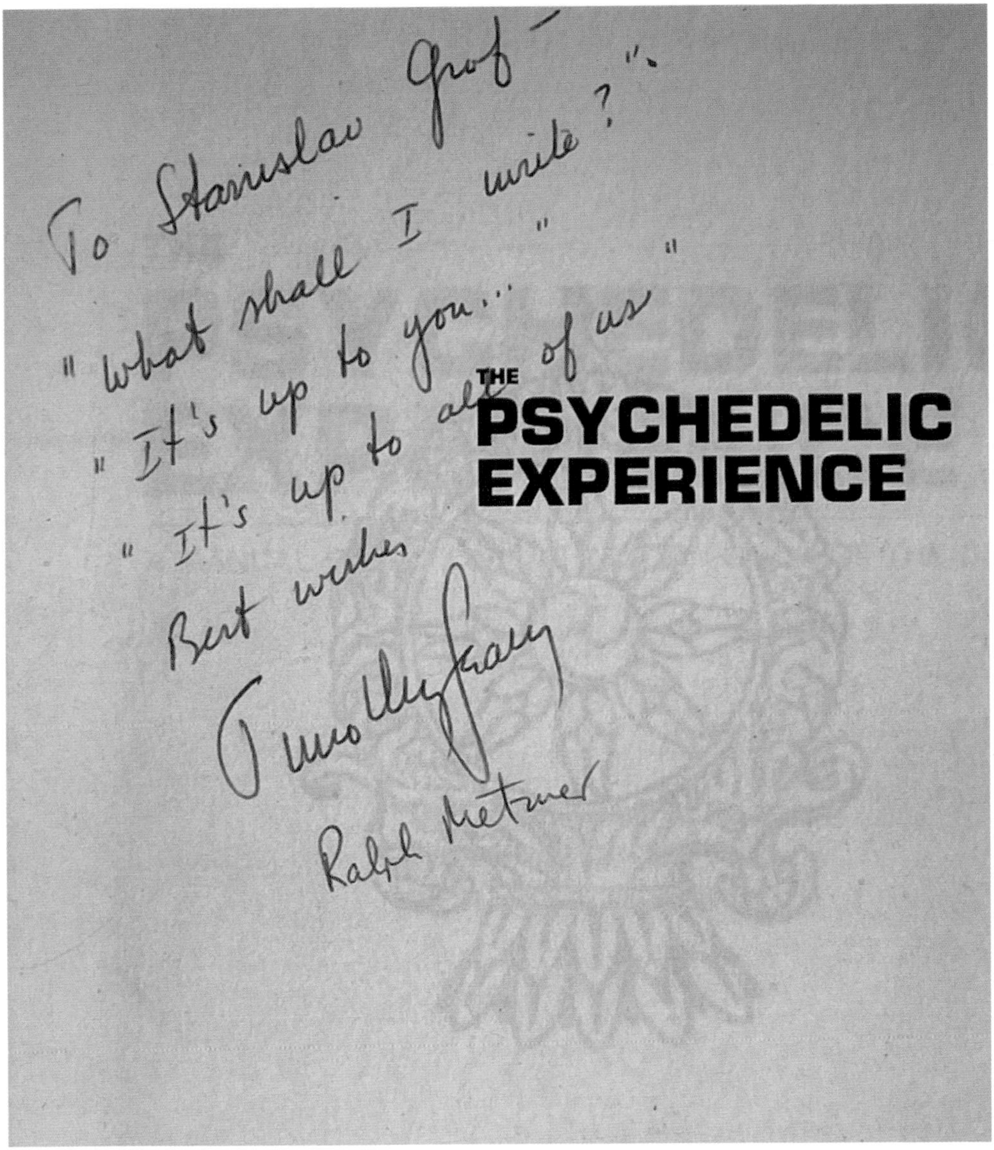

To Stanislav Grof ~

" what shall I write ? "

" It's up to you... "

" It's up to all of us "

THE PSYCHEDELIC EXPERIENCE

Best wishes

Timothy Leary

Ralph Metzner

Personal dedication to Stan Grof by Timothy Leary and Ralph Metzner in Millbrook 1965

Rites of passage initiation ceremony, Kwakiutl Indians, North Pacific coast

and the heights of the superconscious was too threatening for the Puritanical values of Euro-American society. In addition, the irrational and transrational nature of psychedelic experiences seriously challenged the very foundations of the materialistic worldview of Western science. The existence and nature of these experiences could not be explained in the context of mainstream theories and seriously undermined the metaphysical assumptions concerning priority of matter over consciousness on which Western culture is built. It also threatened the leading myth of the industrial world by showing that true fulfillment does not come from achievement of material goals but from a profound mystical experience.

It was not just the culture at large that was unprepared for the psychedelic experience; it was also the helping profession. For most psychiatrists and psychologists, psychotherapy meant disciplined face-to-face discussions or free-associating on the couch. The intense emotions and dramatic physical manifestations in psyche-delic sessions appeared to them to be too close to what they used to associate with psychopathology. It was hard for them to imagine that such states could be healing and transformative. As a result, they did not trust the reports about the extraordinary power of psychedelic psychotherapy coming from those colleagues who had enough courage to take the chances and do psychedelic therapy, or from their clients. To complicate the situation even further, many of the phenomena occurring in psychedelic sessions could not be understood within the context of theories dominating academic thinking. The possibility of reliving birth or episodes from embryonic life, obtaining accurate information about world history and mythology from the collective unconscious, experiencing archetypal realities and karmic memories, or perceiving remote events in out-of-body states, were simply too fantastic to be believable for an average professional. Yet those of us who had the chance to work with LSD and were willing to radically change our theoretical understanding of the psyche and practical strategy of therapy were able to see and appreciate the enormous potential of psychedelics, both as therapeutic tools and as substances of extraordinary heuristic value.

In one of my early books, I suggested that the potential significance of LSD and other psychedelics for psychiatry and psychology was comparable to the value the microscope has for biology and medicine or the telescope has for astronomy. My later experience with psychedelics only confirmed this initial impression. These substances function as unspecific amplifiers that increase the *cathexis* (energetic charge) associated with the deep unconscious contents of the psyche and make them available for conscious processing. This unique property of psychedelics makes it possible to study psychological undercurrents that govern our experiences and behaviors to a depth that cannot be matched by any other method and tool available in modern mainstream psychiatry and psychology. In addition, it offers unique opportunities for healing of emotional and psychosomatic disorders, for positive personality transformation, and consciousness evolution.

Naturally, the tools of this power carry with them greater risks than more conservative and far less effective tools currently accepted and used by mainstream psychiatry, such as verbal psychotherapy or tranquilizing medication. Responsible clinical research has shown that these risks can be minimized by responsible use and careful control of the set and setting. However, legislators responding to unsu-pervised mass use of psychedelics did not get their information from scientific publications, but from the stories of sensation-hunting journalists. The legal and administrative sanctions against psychedelics did not deter lay experimentation, but

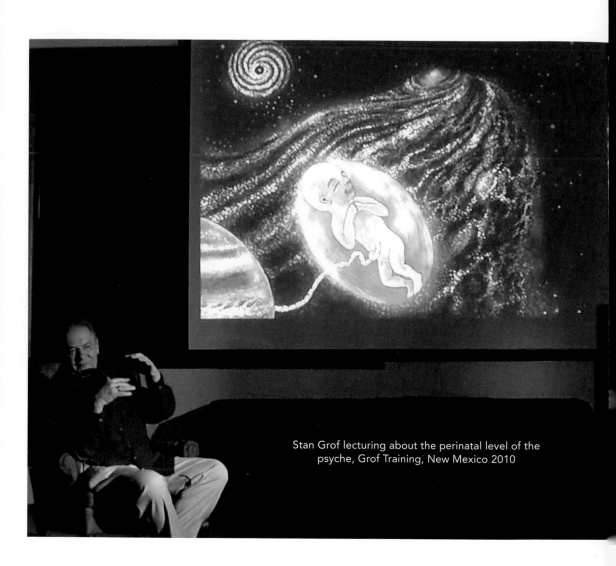

Stan Grof lecturing about the perinatal level of the psyche, Grof Training, New Mexico 2010

they terminated all legitimate scientific research of these substances. By an unfortunate combination of circumstances, Albert Hofmann's wonder child became a "problem child."

For those of us who had the privilege to explore and experience the extraordinary potential of psychedelics, this was a tragic loss for psychiatry, psychology, and psychotherapy. We felt that these unfortunate developments wasted what was probably the single most important opportunity in the history of these disciplines. Had it been possible to avoid the unnecessary mass hysteria and continue responsible research of psychedelics, they could have radically transformed the theory and practice of psychiatry. This research would have brought a new understanding of the psyche and of consciousness that could become an integral part of a comprehensive new scientific paradigm of the twenty-first century.

LSD researchers responded in different ways to the legal and political sanctions against psychedelics. Some of them grudgingly accepted them and reluctantly returned to mainstream therapeutic practices, which now seemed to them boring and painfully ineffective. A few of us attempted to develop non-drug methods for inducing non-ordinary states of consciousness with the experiential spectrum and healing potential comparable to psychedelics. There were also those who saw the extraordinary benefits of LSD psychotherapy and decided not to sacrifice the wellbeing of their clients to irrational and scientifically unsubstantiated legislation, and continued their work in secret.

In addition to the therapeutic value of psychedelics, many of these professionals were also aware of the entheogenic potential of these substances. For this reason, they understood their work with LSD to be not only therapeutic practice, but also religious activity in the best sense of the word. From this perspective, the legal sanctions against psychedelics appeared to be not only unfounded and misguided, but represented a serious infringement of religious freedom guaranteed by the American Constitution.

At present, when more than three decades elapsed since official LSD research was effectively terminated, I can attempt to evaluate the past history of this substance and glimpse into its future. After having personally conducted over the last fifty years more than four thousand psychedelic sessions, I have developed great awe and respect for these substances and their enormous positive, as well as negative potential. They are powerful tools and like any tool they can be used skillfully, ineptly, or destructively. The result will be critically dependent on the set and setting.

The question whether LSD is a phenomenal medicine or a devil's drug makes as little sense as a similar question asked about the positive or negative potential of a knife. Naturally, we will get a very different report from a surgeon who bases his or her judgment on successful operations and from the police chief who investigates murders committed with knives in back alleys of New York City. It would also make little sense to judge the usefulness and dangers of a knife by watching children who play with it without adequate maturity and skill. Similarly, the image of LSD will vary whether we focus on the results of responsible clinical or spiritual use, naive and careless mass self-experimentation of the young generation, or deliberately destructive experiments of the army or the CIA.

Until it is clearly understood that the results of the administration of

Biochemist and psychopharmacologist Sasha Shulgin visited by Stan Grof
in his laboratory in California 2009

psychedelics are critically influenced by the factors of set and setting, there is no hope for rational decisions in regard to psychedelic drug policies. I firmly believe that psychedelics can be used in such a way that the benefits far outweigh the risks. This has been amply proven by millenia of safe ritual and spiritual use of psychedelics by generations of shamans, individual healers, and entire aboriginal cultures.

However, the Western industrial civilization has so far abused nearly all its discoveries and there is not much hope that psychedelics will make an exception, unless we rise as a group to a higher level of consciousness and emotional maturity.

Whether or not psychedelics will return into psychiatry and will again become part of the therapeutic armamentarium is a complex problem and its solution will probably be determined not only by the results of scientific research, but also by a variety of political, legal, economic, and mass-psychological factors.

However, I believe that Western society is at present much better equipped to accept and assimilate psychedelics than it was in the 1950s. At the time when psychiatrists and psychologists started to experiment with LSD, psychotherapy was limited to verbal exchanges between therapist and clients. Intense emotions and active behavior were referred to as "acting-out" and were seen as violations of basic therapeutic rules. Psychedelic sessions were on the other side of the spectrum, evoking dramatic emotions, psychomotor excitement, and vivid perceptual changes. They thus seemed to be more like states that psychiatrists considered pathological and tried to suppress by all means than conditions to which one would attribute therapeutic potential. This was reflected in the terms "hallucinogens," "delirogens," "psychotomimetics," and "experimental psychoses," used initially for psychedelics and the states induced by them. In any case, psychedelic sessions more resembled scenes from anthropological movies about healing rituals of "primitive" cultures and other ceremonies than those expected in a psychoanalyst's office.

In addition, many of the experiences and observations from psychedelic sessions seemed to seriously challenge the image of the human psyche and of the universe developed by Newtonian-Cartesian science and considered to be accurate and definitive descriptions of "objective reality." Psychedelic subjects reported experiential identification with other people, animals, and various aspects of nature, during which they gained access to new information about areas about which they previously had no intellectual knowledge. The same was true about experiential excursions into the lives of their human and animal ancestors, as well as racial, collective, and karmic memories.

On occasion, this new information was drawn from experiences involving reliving biological birth and memories of prenatal life, encounters with archetypal beings, and visits to mythological realms of different cultures of the world. In out-of-body experiences, experimental subjects were able to witness and accurately describe remote events occurring in locations that were outside of the range of their senses. None of these happenings were considered possible in the context of traditional materialistic science, and yet, in psychedelic sessions, they were observed frequently. This naturally caused deep conceptual turmoil and confusion in the minds of conventionally trained experimenters. Under these circumstances, many professionals chose to stay away from this area to preserve their scientific worldview and to protect their common sense and sanity.

Stan Grof and Fritz Perls at Esalen 1965

The last three decades have brought many revolutionary changes that have profoundly influenced the climate in the world of psychotherapy. Humanistic and transpersonal psychologies have developed powerful experiential techniques that emphasize deep regression, direct expression of intense emotions, and body-work leading to release of physical energies. Among these new approaches to self-exploration are Gestalt practice, bioenergetics and other neo-Reichian methods, primal therapy, rebirthing, and holotropic breathwork. The inner experiences and outer manifestations, as well as therapeutic strategies, in these therapies bear a great similarity to those observed in psychedelic sessions. These non-drug therapeutic strategies involve a similar spectrum of experiences, as well as comparable conceptual challenges. As a result, for therapists practicing along these lines, the introduction of psychedelics would represent the next logical step rather than dramatic change in their practice.

The culture at large shows encouraging signs as well. Grassroots movements around birth and death, for example, reveal a growing discontent with the sanitization of powerful experiences. Today, midwives can be state certified and home births are increasingly popular, whereas in the 1950s these were considered backward or primitive. People can choose to die at home, thanks to the hospice movement, instead of in sterile hospital settings. Previously eccentric healing techniques, like massage and acupuncture, are widely accepted, even by health insurance plans. Eastern spiritual practices have moved to the mainstream of Western culture, with meditation centers and yoga schools to be found in every major city. Increasingly, the authority of traditional medical science, with its firm separation between mind and body, is becoming suspect, and people are seeking more holistic alternatives. These shifts may signal that society is more ready for psychedelics today.

Moreover, the Newtonian-Cartesian thinking in science, which in the 1960s enjoyed great authority and popularity, has been progressively undermined by astonishing developments in a variety of disciplines. This has happened to such an extent that an increasing number of scientists feel an urgent need for an entirely different worldview, a new scientific paradigm. Salient examples of this development are philosophical implications of quantum relativistic physics, David Bohm's theory of holomovement, Karl Pribram's holographic theory of the brain, Ilya Prigogine's theory of dissipative structures, Rupert Sheldrake's theory of morphogenetic fields, Gregory Bateson's brilliant synthesis of systems and information theory, cybernetics, anthropology, and psychology, and particularly Ervin Laszlo's concept of the akashic field, his connectivity hypothesis, and his "integral theory of everything." It is very encouraging to see that all these new developments that are in irreconcilable conflict with traditional science seem to be compatible with the findings of psychedelic research and with transpersonal psychology.

Even more encouraging than the changes in the general scientific climate is the fact that, in a few cases, researchers of the younger generation in the United States and abroad have in recent years been able to obtain official permission to start programs of psychedelic therapy, involving LSD, psilocybin, dimethyltryptamine (DMT), methylenedioxymethamphetamine (MDMA), and ketamine. I hope that this is the beginning of a renaissance of interest in psychedelic research that will eventually return these extraordinary tools into the hands of responsible therapists. I personally believe that in the future LSD will be seen as one of the most influential discoveries of the twentieth century and that Albert Hofmann's "problem child" will again be seen—as it should have been seen all along—as a "wonder child" that had to grow up in a dysfunctional society.

I would like to end this foreword on a personal note. Writing it gives me the opportunity to express my profound gratitude to Albert Hofmann for everything that his discovery brought into my personal and professional life and the lives of countless others who used his gift responsibly and with respect that this extraordinary tool deserves. I have had the privilege to know Albert personally and meet him repeatedly on various occasions. Over the years, I have developed great affection and deep admiration for him, not only as an outstanding scientist, but also as an extraordinary human being. After what will soon be a century of a full, blessed, and productive life, he radiates amazing vitality, curiosity, and love for all creation.

I had another opportunity to meet Albert during my recent visit in Switzerland, where I was teaching an advanced training module on holotropic breathwork entitled *Fantastic Art*. It was held in the H. R. Giger Museum in Gruyères and Albert came as a guest of honor.

After we had lunch and enjoyed a guided tour through the museum, during which he braved three floors of steep stairs, he sat down with our group for a discussion, which turned into his passionate apotheosis of the beauty and mystery of creation. He spoke about the miraculous chemistry that gives rise to the pigments responsible for the colors of flowers and butterfly wings, about the gratitude he felt for being alive and participating in consciousness, and about the need to embrace creation in its totality, including its shadow side, because without polarity the universe we live in could not have been created. When he left, we all felt that we just had attended a darshan with a spiritual teacher. It was clear that Albert had joined the group of great scientists—like Albert Einstein and Isaac Newton—for whom rigorous pursuit of their discipline brought the recognition of the miraculous divine order underlying the world of matter and the natural phenomena. I would like to use this opportunity to wish him all the best for his forthcoming auspicious hundredth anniversary and hope that we will enjoy his presence in the world for many more years.

Swiss fantastic realist Hans Ruedi Giger guiding Albert Hofmann and Stan Grof
through his museum in Gruyères 2005

Albert Hofmann four months before his death, January 2008

Gallery

Stan, Brigitte, and Rick Tarnas in China, January 2016

Holotropic breathwork group, China, January 2016

Talks about art, ITA Conference, Prague, September 2017

Brigitte, Stan, Paul Grof, and Mary Pearson in Prague 2017

Javier Charme, Stan Grof, Brigitte Grof, and Viktoria Luchetti, workshop in Argentina, February 2018

California Institute of Integral Studies

The Trustees of the University upon the recommendation of the Faculty

hereby confer upon

STANISLAV GROF

the degree of

Doctor of Humane Letters

Psychedelic Therapy and Healing Arts

Honoris Causa

by virtue of exemplary fulfillment of all requirements prescribed therefor together with all the rights and privileges pertaining thereto.

Given at San Francisco, this Nineteenth day of May, Two Thousand Eighteen

President of the Institute

Chair, Board of Trustees

Stan receives honorary degree from CIIS, San Francisco, May 2018

Stan and Brigitte in Esalen, May 2018

Holotropic breathwork and gender reconciliation workshop in Esalen with Diane Haug, Will Keepin, Cynthia Brix, Stan and Brigitte Grof, May 2018

Stan signing his Psychonaut books
in Mill Valley, California, 2019

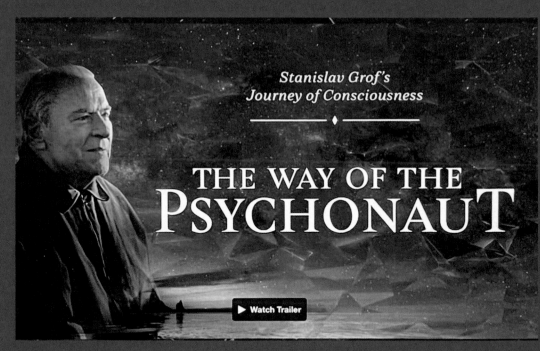

Launch of the film *The Way of the Psychonaut*, San Francisco, August 2019

Filmmaker Susan Hess Logeais and Stan Grof working on the documentary
The Way of the Psychonaut, Mill Valley 2018

At the Symposium 75 Years of LSD in Münchenstein near Basel, Switzerland, 2018

HOME   HOLOTROPIC STATES   HISTORY   INTERNATIONAL TRAININGS   NEWS & EVENTS   GALLERY | BOOKS | VIDEOS   PSYCHONAUT

GROF® LEGACY TRAINING

Launch of the new international Grof® Legacy Training, May 2020

Jack Kornfield, Brigitte and Stan Grof, 2016

Visiting Ram Dass in Maui 2016

Michael Harner with Stan, Mill Valley, California 2016

Rick Tarnas, Brigitte and Stan Grof, California 2016

Stan Grof and Jack Kornfield, California, August 2016

Rick Doblin visiting Stan and Brigitte at their home in Mill Valley, California 2019

Paul and Stan Grof, Mill Valley, August 2018

Stan in Big Sur 2017

Stan in Prague 2017

Stan in Peru 2018

Stan in Mauritius 2019

Stan on Easter Island 2016

Stan in China 2015

*Stan is love—*Stanislav!

My Explorations of LSD: From Pharmacology to Archetypes

Stan Grof about his life's work
Interview by Brigitte Grof

Stan Grof at
Esalen 2018

BRIGITTE: **Stan, your two volumes of *The Way of the Psychonaut* is a compendium of more than sixty years of your research with LSD. When you began, it was a new substance and almost nothing was known about it. As the new understanding of LSD was emerging, it was necessary to change and make additions to a number of areas in the old paradigm of psychiatry. As time went on, it was also necessary to make ongoing revisions in your own understanding of the effects of LSD. It would be interesting to review these stages in your understanding.**

STAN: I have been interested in and exploring the effects of psychedelic substances and other non-ordinary states of consciousness for more than sixty-five years, my entire adult life. My understanding of LSD changed dramatically several times during these years. Can you imagine what it was like when this new, extraordinary substance of formidable potency fell into our lap? LSD was an entirely new substance, created for the first time by chemical synthesis. As far as we know, LSD does not exist anywhere in a pure form in nature—although it can be derived from the ergot alkaloids created by the fungus *Claviceps purpurea*—and its psychoactive power is without parallel. We were experimenting with our patients and self-experimenting on ourselves; there was no precedent for these experiences and every new session represented another major surprise. We were involved in explorations of entirely new worlds and delving into them was a series of amazing adventures.

As the research continued, new discoveries emerged that required us to change our perspectives and create new concepts. The major changes in my understanding of LSD can be divided into several periods:

1. Psychopharmacological Laboratory Research
2. Psycholytic Psychotherapy—Postnatal Experiences and COEX Systems
3. A New Cartography of the Psyche—Perinatal Experiences (BPMs I-IV*)
4. Transpersonal Experiences and World Mythology
5. Archetypes and the Archetypal Cosmology

How and when did you start working with LSD?

In the fourth year of my medical studies, I worked as a volunteer in the Prague Psychiatric Clinic. My preceptor, Dr. George Roubíček, received complimentary LSD-25 (Delysid) from Sandoz, the pharmaceutical company from Basel, Switzerland. Dr. Roubíček was very interested in this substance, but its sessions lasted many hours and he did not have time in his busy schedule to follow his clients personally.

To my great disappointment, our medical and psychological students were not allowed to volunteer in LSD sessions like the students at Harvard University. But Roubíček was very happy to use his students as gofers. During the last two years of my university studies, I spent my free time at the Psychiatric Clinic helping with the LSD sessions, supervising his experimental subjects, and writing notes about the sessions. Among the subjects were psychiatrists and psychologists, artists, philosophers, and scientists. As I was listening to their fantastic stories, my palate was deeply whetted and I could not wait to be able to experience "Hofmann's Elixir" myself.

When did you finally get to do an LSD session yourself?

I experienced my first LSD session on November 13, 1956. Dr. Roubíček was at that time very interested in electroencephalography (EEG) and more specifically in "driving the brain waves" (or "entraining" the brain waves). This experiment involved exposing patients to strong stroboscopic light of different frequencies and finding out if this would influence the brain waves of their suboccipital area.

*BPM refers to Basic Perinatal Matrices

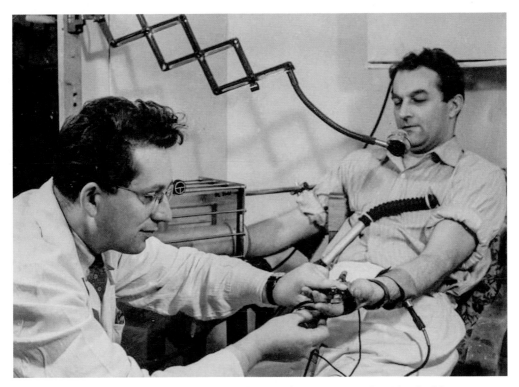

Miloš Vojtěchovský, a psychiatrist and pharmacologist, prepares Stanislav Grof for an LSD experiment in the Pharmacological Institute in Prague 1956

Dr. Roubíček asked all the volunteers who wanted to experience LSD to accept this procedure before, during, and after their sessions. My guide for this first session was my younger brother Paul, who was a student in medical school and was also very interested in psychiatry. We started the experiment at 8:00 a.m.; I was given an ampoule of Sandoz Delysid. I started feeling the effect of the LSD about forty-five minutes after ingestion; it was first a slight malaise, lightheadedness, and nausea.

Then these vegetative symptoms disappeared and were replaced by a fantastic display of colorful, brilliant abstract and geometrical visions unfolding in rapid kaleidoscopic sequences. Some of them resembled exquisite stained glass, windows in medieval Gothic cathedrals, others more like arabesques from Muslim mosques. To describe the exquisite nature of these visions, I made a reference to Scheherazade's *One Thousand and One Nights*. At the time, I thought that these mosaic images were created by the structure of the rods and cones in my retinas. Later when I read Benoît Mandelbrot's work, I realized that my psyche had created a wild array of fractal images, similar to the graphic representations of nonlinear equations that can be created by modern computers.

As the session continued, the experience moved deeper into my unconscious psyche. It is difficult to find words for the intoxicating fugue of emotions, visions, and illuminating insights about my life and into existence in general. It was so profound and shattering that it instantly overshadowed my previous interest in Freudian psychoanalysis. I could not believe how much I learned in those few hours. However, all that paled in comparison with what was yet to come. Between the third and fourth hour of my session, when the effect of the LSD was culminating, Dr. Roubíček's research assistant appeared and announced that it was time for the EEG experiment. She took me to a small chamber, carefully pasted electrodes on my scalp, and asked me to lie down and close my eyes. She then placed a giant stroboscopic light above my head and turned it on.

This combination of LSD and stroboscopic light triggered in me a phenomenal experience of Cosmic Consciousness that profoundly transformed my personal and professional life. I decided to dedicate the rest of my life to this phenomenon of mystical transcendence, which Rudolf Otto termed *Mysterium tremendum et fascinans*. Since that time, the research and study of non-ordinary states of consciousness has been my profession, vocation, and passion.

It is now the year 2021 and sixty-five years since your determined decision to pursue research in non-ordinary states of consciousness or what you would later term holotropic ("moving toward wholeness") states—those states that have a therapeutic, transformative, heuristic, and evolutionary potential. How did your psychedelic research begin?

When LSD appeared in the scientific world, the researchers thought that the secret of this substance was in chemistry and pharmacology. I made a connection with Miloš Vojtěchovský, a psychiatrist and pharmacologist, who had access to psychedelics through several research institutes in Prague. I worked under his guidance together with two biochemists, Vladimír Vítek and Karel Ryšánek, and the psychologist Eva Horáčková. We invited a group of scientists who were interested in psychedelics, including psychiatrists, psychologists, pharmacologists, chemists, and biologists.

We had LSD-25 (Delysid) and psilocybin from Sandoz in Switzerland, and mescaline from Pfizer in Germany. We experimented also with psychedelics with a very short duration of effect: adrenochrome and adrenolutine from Abram Hoffer and Humphry Osmond from Canada and dimethyl-, diethyl-, and dipropyltryptamine (DMT, DET, and DPT), gifts from the chemist and psychiatrist Stephen Szára and his colleague Zoltán Böszörmény from Budapest, Hungary.

Our project had a rich array of examinations; we administered every hour on the hour samples of blood and urine, a battery of psychological tests, electro-encephalography (EEG), blood pressure, pulse rate, skin resistance, and chromatography. Our experimental subjects stayed for a full day in the institute and received in a double-blind way either various psychedelic substances or a placebo. The psychedelics with a short duration of effect required appropriately less testing time.

We then selected from the psychiatric department a number of volunteer schizophrenic patients matched by gender, age, IQ, and other variables and brought them for a day into our institute and performed the same testing with them. The question was whether our experimental subjects would show during their psychedelic sessions some of the parameters we found in our schizophrenic patients.

Vojtěchovský's research contributed to the pharmacology of psychedelic substances, but none of these findings had any relevance to the understanding of schizophrenia. The set and setting of this project focused on biological exploration and was not conducive to introspective observation. In spite of it, I was able to notice between the short intervals of testing that our subjects showed remarkable intervariability in their responses to the psychedelic substances.

The same substance, with the same dose and in the same set and setting, showed a wide range of manifestations. One person experienced depression, another a hypomanic mood and was irritable or aggressive. Some people had mostly physical reactions, such as extremely cold feelings, nausea, or headache. Visual experiences ranged between optical illusions, colorful geometric images, synesthesias, visions of memories from childhood, or various persons, animals, or landscapes. In spite of frequent testing and examinations that left very little time for introspection, several people had glances of mystical experiences.

I also discovered that a person who later ingested the same substance showed an equally wide range of intraindividual variability. It is known that the results of psychological tests remain by and large the same for people during a sequence of repetitions. However, when we took LSD or psilocybin, twice with the same dose two weeks apart, the results could be completely different. As a result of these observations, it became obvious that we were not really studying pharmacology.

The existence of pharmacology requires predictability in the results of administration of specific substances. If we use a specific pharmacon, for example penicillin, an anesthetic, apomorphine, or insulin, we expect a consistent result.

With LSD or psilocybin, we had no idea what the result would be. I realized that these medicines were substances of a completely different kind than the usual pharmacons. In my first book, *Realms of the Human Unconscious,* I wrote that, properly used, LSD has the potential to become for psychiatry as important as the microscope is in medicine or the telescope in astronomy. At this point, I lost interest in pharmacology and decided to explore LSD and psilocybin in psychotherapy and clinical research.

Your interest moved from psychoanalysis to psychedelics. It is interesting that Freud wrote a passage in his *General Introduction to Psychoanalysis* that was very interesting and in today's renaissance of psychedelic research sounds prophetic—a chemical substance might in the future help psychoanalysis to become a "causal therapy in the true sense of the word": "*Supposing, now, that it were possible, by some chemical means, perhaps, to interfere in this mechanism, to increase or diminish the quantity of libido present at a given time or to strengthen one instinct at the cost of another—this then would be a causal therapy in the true sense of the word, for which our analysis would have carried out the indispensable preliminary work of reconnaissance.*"(FREUD 1943)

Freud was a genius in many ways and this prophetic passage is certainly remarkable. I will discuss later how psychotherapy with LSD can greatly expand and deepen Freud's pioneering ideas. My initial psychedelic therapy was inspired by the insights of psychoanalysis; this method was called *psycholytic therapy,* a term coined by Ronald Sandison in England, which means literally "soul-dissolving" or "dissolving conflicts in the mind." The psycholytic approach was popular among European psychiatrists and psychologists, while less so among American and Canadian professionals. It involved administering a long series of medium dosages of LSD (100–250 mcg). The clients were allowed to keep their eyes open and talk frequently with the therapists.

During the early years when I used this method, I discovered some important insights into the human psyche, the therapeutic process, and the dynamics of LSD and psilocybin. But I realized that psycholytic therapy also had some important disadvantages. The lower dosages, opening of one's eyes, and talking during the session significantly slowed down the therapeutic process. To improve the therapeutic results, I decided to use higher dosages, play hi-fi music, and ask my patients to use eyeshades and talk only when it was necessary.

When I first immigrated to the United States in 1967, I worked at the Maryland Psychiatric Research Center. We used with our patients larger

Maryland Psychedelic Research Center, Spring Grove, Baltimore

dosages—400–600 mcg ("a single overwhelming dose")—an approach that was more popular in the U.S. and Canada. Our clients were alcoholics, narcotic addicts, neurotics, terminal cancer patients, and mental health professionals. We were using LSD and entheogens such as MDA and dipropyltryptamine (DPT) and, unlike in psycholytic therapy, we were allowed to administer only three sessions.

The psycholytic approach also had some advantages. To use lower dosages and allow patients to keep their eyes open made it possible to study optical and acoustic illusions. I recorded a long list of such illusions—personages, animals, and mythological creatures. I analyzed these images and tried to understand why certain patients saw me during their sessions at certain times transformed into a silverback gorilla, a powerful magician, Adolf Hitler, a black panther, Supreme Court judge, Siberian shaman, mass murderer, angry toddler, cowboy with a lasso, or Aladdin with a magic lamp.

I also wanted to understand why my patients' treatment room looked at various times to them like a cottage on an island in the Pacific Ocean, a concentration camp or death row, a medieval alchemist's laboratory, the Garden of Eden, or a bordello. The sound of steps of people walking behind the door of the treatment room were perceived at times to come from the heavy boots of SS officers, or the humming of the air-conditioner in the room was transformed into "La Marseillaise" or the hocketing of Congolese Pygmies. I was able to find the deeper meaning in these optical and acoustic illusions: they represent overdetermined, emotionally charged memories, which can be understood in the way similar to Freud's analysis of dreams. These psychedelic illusions and projections—like dreams—can be excellent therapeutic tools. I gave a number of examples of this understanding in my first book *Realms of the Human Unconscious*. Essentially, clients will tend to project onto the world around them elements and sounds that convey the emotional character of the material that is emerging from their psyches.

You mentioned Freud and free associations. What differences do you see between working with LSD—and other holotropic states of consciousness—and verbal psychotherapy?
The postnatal level of the psyche is well known and explored in traditional psychology and psychotherapy. However, there are several important differences between exploring this domain in verbal psychotherapy and working with holotropic states of consciousness. The first difference is that one does not just remember emotionally significant events or reconstruct them indirectly from dreams, slips of the tongue, or from transference distortions. In holotropic states of consciousness, one can experience the original emotions, physical sensations, and even sensory perceptions in full age regression.

This means that during the reliving of an important trauma from infancy or childhood, the individual actually experiences the body image, physical sensations, naive perception of the world, and emotions corresponding to the age that he or she was at that time. The authenticity of this regression is supported by the fact that the wrinkles in the face of these people temporarily disappear, giving them an infantile expression, and their gestures and postures can resemble those of children.

The second difference between work with holotropic states of consciousness and verbal psychotherapy is the discovery that unresolved physical shocks and threats can be very important psychotraumas. These include serious operations, accidents, and children's diseases. Particularly important is the distress associated with suffocation, strangling, and choking, such as experiences of near drowning, diphtheria, croup, whooping cough, or aspiration of a foreign object. These disorders do not respond to verbal therapy; they require that the patient relives and resolves the underlying pains and blocks in holotropic states of consciousness. These psychotraumas of physical origin play a major role in the genesis of many emotional and psychosomatic disorders, such as migraine headaches, psychogenic asthma, phobias, sadomasochistic tendencies, depression, or suicidal tendencies. Reliving of such traumatic memories and their integration can have very beneficial effects.

What do you mean by the term inner healing intelligence of the psyche that can be observed in LSD therapy or holotropic breathwork sessions?

The psycholytic approach allows us to explore sequential layers of the unconscious psyche. My patients called this process "onion peeling" or "chemo-archeology of the psyche." The effect of LSD or psilocybin engages an "inner radar," a mechanism that unfetters in a selective way contents of the unconscious that are close to the surface and have a very powerful emotional charge (Freud's cathexis). In other words psychedelics activate the symptoms or syndromes that are currently most unpleasant and difficult for the patients. This mechanism brings these symptoms spontaneously to the surface for their full processing and resolution.

Work with this inner healing intelligence ("inner radar") offers great advantages in comparison with verbal psychotherapy. In verbal therapy the client presents a broad array of information of various kinds and the therapist has to decide what is important, what is irrelevant, where the client is blocking, and so on. Since there is no general agreement about basic theoretical issues among the different psychological schools and approaches, such assessments will always reflect the personal bias of the therapist, as well as the specific views and biases of his or her school.

Your work with psycholytic therapy and what your patients called "peeling the onion of the psyche" also made it possible to discover what you call COEX systems? Can you describe what they are?

The important insight that emerged from my psycholytic therapy was that emotionally charged memories are not stored in the unconscious as a mosaic of isolated imprints but, rather, form complex dynamic constellations. I coined for these memory systems the term COEX systems, short for *systems of condensed experience.* A COEX system consists of emotionally charged memories from different periods of our life that share similar emotions or physical sensations.

Each COEX has a basic experiential theme that permeates all its layers and represents their common denominator. A particular COEX system might contain all the major memories of humiliating, degrading, and shaming experiences that have damaged our self-esteem. In another COEX, the common denominator

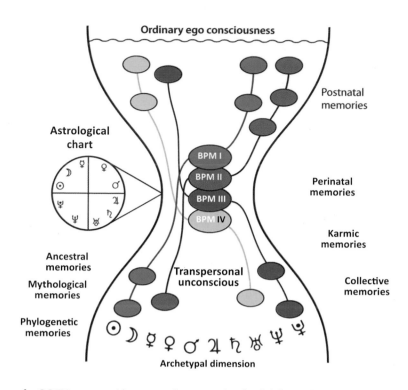

Diagram of a COEX system with postnatal memory levels of different life phases (upper part) and transpersonal experiences (karmic, ancestral, and tribal memories)

can be anxiety experienced in various shocking and terrifying situations, or claustrophobic and suffocating feelings from various oppressive and confining events. Another common motif is rejection and emotional deprivation that damaged our ability to trust men, women, peers, or people in general. Situations that have generated profound feelings of guilt, shame, or a sense of failure, events that have left us with a conviction that sex is dangerous or disgusting, or encounters with indiscriminate aggression and violence are also characteristic examples. Particularly important are COEX systems that contain memories of encounters with situations endangering life, health, and the integrity of the body. The individual layers of a COEX then contains inflections and variations on the basic theme of the COEX that occurred at different periods of the person's life. This observation of variations of experience based around a common theme resembles Richard Wagner's idea of the Leitmotif.

The above discussion could easily leave the impression that COEX systems always contain traumatic and painful memories. However, it is the intensity of the experience and its emotional relevance that determines whether a memory will be included into a COEX, not its unpleasant nature. In addition to negative constellations, there are also those that comprise memories of very pleasant or even ecstatic moments. Examples are blissful prenatal experiences, being nursed by a loving mother, falling in love, exciting times in beautiful scenery during family vacations, listening or playing beautiful music, or scuba diving around tropical islands.

We have so far talked about the postnatal level of the psyche—recollective memories and Freud's individual unconscious. This is essentially the realm described by the current understanding in psychiatry. You added the discoveries of the "inner radar" and inner intelligence of the psyche, the layering of the psyche, the COEX systems, and the importance of physical insults as psychotraumas. How did people's experiences progress when their course of therapy and self-exploration continued?

When the process of deep experiential therapy and self-exploration moved beyond the level of memories from childhood and infancy, my clients started encountering emotions and physical sensations of extreme intensity, often surpassing anything they previously considered possible. At this point, the experiences became a strange mixture of being born and dying. They involved a sense of severe, life-threatening confinement, pain, anxiety, crushing, choking, and a desperate and determined struggle to free oneself and survive. The extreme suffering formed a characteristic triad: being crazy, dying, and never escaping out of this hellish realm. Sooner or later, my patients realized that this process was the reliving of their own biological birth. To my astonishment, I separately confirmed this in my own LSD sessions.

I coined for these experiences the term *perinatal*. It is a Greek-Latin composite word in which the prefix *peri* means "near" or "around" and the root *natalis* signifies "pertaining to childbirth." This word is commonly used in medicine to describe various biological processes occurring shortly before, during, and immediately after birth. For example, obstetricians talk about perinatal hemorrhage, infection, or brain damage. However, according to traditional medicine, the fetus does not consciously experience birth and the event is not recorded in its memory. Clinicians and academicians thus never hear about perinatal experiences. The use of the term perinatal in connection with consciousness reflects my own findings and is entirely new.*

The official position of academic psychiatry is that biological birth does not constitute a psychotrauma that can be remembered. The usual reason for denying

*Grof, *Realms of the Human Unconscious* and Grof, "Tentative Theoretical Framework for Understanding Dynamics of LSD Psychotherapy."

Stan Grof giving a lecture about the perinatal
level of the psyche, New Mexico 2010

the possibility of birth memory is that the neurons in the cerebral cortex of the newborn are not yet fully "myelinized"—which means not completely covered with the protective sheaths of a fatty substance called *myelin*. Surprisingly, this same argument is not used to deny the existence and importance of memories from the time of nursing, a period that immediately follows birth. The psychological significance of the experiences of nursing and even bonding—the exchange of looks and physical contact between the mother and child immediately after birth—is generally recognized and acknowledged by mainstream obstetricians, pediatricians, and child psychiatrists.

After a long avalanche of evidence, I became convinced that we carry in our unconscious the memories of the biological birth process. I also identified four broad clusters of experience that tend to emerge when people are facing this layer of their psyches, for which I coined the term *Basic Perinatal Matrices,* or BPMs I-IV. The four perinatal matrices are related to the consecutive four stages of the birth process.

When we talked about the postnatal level of the psyche, it was your clients reliving of memories from infancy, childhood, teenage years, and adulthood. Part of these memories resembled images from the material world, similar to photographs or movies. Which form did memories take during the unfolding of the perinatal matrices, the memories of the passage through the birth canal? During most of the birth process (the BPMs I-III) the fetus is inside the mother's body.

This is an excellent question. As soon as I discovered the BPMs and realized that they were records or reflections of the memories of the fetus during the stages of birth, I ran into several major problems. Images in holotropic state of consciousness include the fetal body, the amnion membrane, the placenta, and the umbilical cord. These visual perceptions are also accompanied by sounds coming from the inside of the body of the mother or the fetus and from the external world. The dominant physical elements of the birth experience are intense pressures, extreme pains, anxiety, suffocation, and sometimes nausea. Before the onset of the birth and after its completion there could also be periods involving blissful and ecstatic states. The nature of these experiences depends on the stage of the birth process (BPM) and on its course and condition. It is important to emphasize that during the LSD sessions, it is possible to see the fetus inside of the uterus and inside of the pelvis, while in the material world, the fetus could see only the events after birth (BPM IV). And yet, it is possible to see the fetus's face, body, placenta, and the umbilical cord clearly in the perinatal sequences.

In addition, in each of the perinatal matrices, the fetal memories tend to be accompanied by rich symbolic imagery—various personages, animals, mythological

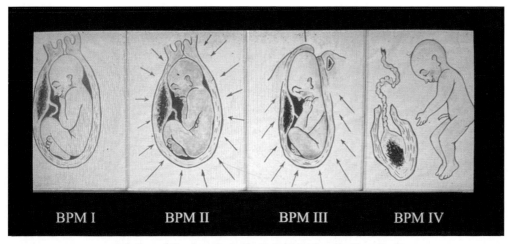

| BPM I | BPM II | BPM III | BPM IV |

Painting of the four Basic Perinatal Matrices by Stan Grof

Amniotic universe, painting from a high dose LSD session by Stan Grof

beings, and natural scenes that match the particular thematic flavor of that BPM. The perinatal experiences form a rich spectrum, only part of which portrays the fetus in the process of childbirth. And the connections between the experiences of the stages of birth and these various symbolic images are not arbitrary and random. The associations are very specific and consistent, yet they are not understandable in terms of conventional logic. Rather than being based on some formal external similarity, they are connected by the fact that they share the same emotional feelings and physical sensations. They have their own deep ordering that can best be referred to as "experiential logic."

Can you show me specific examples of this interplay between the situation of the fetus in the stages of the perinatal matrices and the symbolic imagery linked to them through experiential logic?

For example, the first perinatal matrix (BPM I) portrays the primal union with the mother, the intrauterine existence before the onset of delivery. The experiential situation of this state can be referred to as the *amniotic universe.* When we identify with the fetus in the womb, we do not have an awareness of boundaries and do not differentiate between the inner and the outer. The quality of this experience of unity then depends on the emotional and physical condition of the mother.

The symbolic images during episodes of undisturbed embryonic existence typically portray experiences of vast regions with no boundaries of space or time—interstellar space, galaxies, or the entire universe. Related experiences include floating in the sea, identifying with various aquatic animals, such as fish,

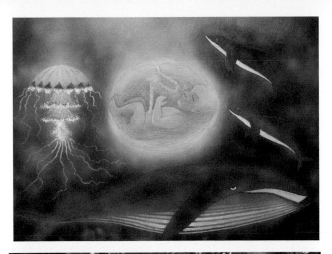

Oceanic womb, painting
from a high dose LSD
session by Stan Grof

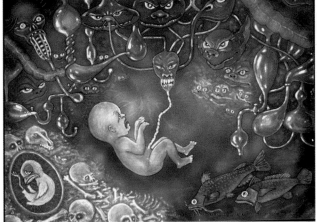

Toxic womb, painting
from a high dose LSD
session by Stan Grof

jellyfish, anemones, algae, dolphins, and whales, or even becoming the ocean. This seems to reflect the fact that the fetus is essentially an aquatic creature. Positive intrauterine experiences can also be associated with visions of nature—safe, beautiful, and unconditionally nourishing like a good womb—or even Mother Nature or Gaia. Mythological images in this perinatal matrix include various celestial realms and paradises as they are described in the mythologies of cultures around the world. I called this type of ecstasy associated with BPM I *Apollonian* or *oceanic;* it is characterized by the transcendence of time and space, feelings of peace, tranquility, clarity, and cosmic unity. Note that none of these symbolic images—the astronomical universe, oceanic life, or mythological figures and abodes—can be derived or explained from memories of biological birth.

When we are reliving episodes of intrauterine disturbances—memories of the "toxic womb" or "bad womb"—we can have the sense of a pervading dark and ominous threat and may feel that we are being poisoned, a very strong source of paranoid ideation. Symbolic images portray polluted waters and toxic dumps.

Contractions are experienced as archetypal predatory birds attacking the fetus, painting from a high dose LSD session by Stan Grof

Onset of delivery experienced as engulfment by a giant maelstrom, painting from a high dose LSD session by Stan Grof

Sequences of this kind can be associated with visions of frightening demonic entities or with a sense of insidious all-pervading evil. Those of us who are reliving episodes of intense or violent interference in prenatal life, such as an imminent miscarriage or attempted abortion, often experience a sense of universal threat or bloody apocalyptic visions of the end of the world.

The second perinatal matrix (BPM II) can be called Cosmic Engulfment, No Exit, or Hell. At the beginning of biological birth, the fetus loses the comfort of the mother's womb and often the protection of the amniotic fluid. The powerful uterine contractions also compress the oxygen-supplying arteries, which are wound through the uterine walls. When we are reliving the onset of delivery, we can feel that we are being sucked into a great whirlpool or maelstrom engulfing the entire world. Other symbolic images include giant devouring or entangling monsters, such as leviathans, dragons, whales, snakes, tarantulas, or octopuses. The sense of overwhelming vital threat can lead to panic anxiety and general mistrust bordering on paranoia. Another experiential variety of the beginning of the second matrix is the theme of descending into the depths of the underworld, the realm of death, or hell. As Joseph Campbell so eloquently described, this is a universal motif in the mythologies of the hero's journey.

In the fully developed first stage of biological birth (BPM II), the uterine contractions periodically constrict the fetus, and the cervix is not yet open. Each

Contractions experienced as an attack of an Octopus-like creature,
painting from a high dose LSD session by Stan Grof

contraction causes compression of the uterine arteries, as we saw, and the fetus is threatened by lack of oxygen. Reliving this stage of birth is one of the worst experiences we can encounter during self-exploration in holotropic states of consciousness. We can feel caught in a monstrous claustrophobic nightmare with enormous hydraulic pressures, exposed to agonizing emotional and physical pain, and have a sense of utter helplessness and hopelessness, feelings of loneliness, guilt, the absurdity of life.

A person in this predicament typically loses his or her sense of linear time and becomes convinced that this situation will never end, and that there is absolutely no way out. The characteristic perceptions of this experiential triad include dying, going crazy, and never coming back. While under the influence of this matrix, we are selectively blinded and unable to see anything positive in our life or in human existence in general. Under the influence of this state of mind, existential philosophy appears to be the only true description of reality or valid strategy.

Reliving this stage of birth—BPM II—is usually accompanied by symbolic images, including various people, animals, or even mythological beings trapped in a painful and hopeless predicament similar to that of the fetus caught in the

Archetypal figure of the Devouring Mother Goddess as giant spider,
painting from a high dose LSD session by Stan Grof

relentless grip of the contracting uterus. We can experience the tortures of sinners in hell, the agony of Jesus on the cross, or the excruciating torments of Greek mythological figures representing endless suffering, such as Sisyphus, Prometheus, or Tantalus. These symbolic visions that accompany the fetal images cannot be produced and explained as memories of the biological birth; they are connected to birth by the similarity of the emotions and sensations involved.

The third perinatal matrix (BPM III) portrays the Death-Rebirth Struggle during the second clinical stage of biological delivery. The cervix dilates and opens and the fetus descends into the pelvis. The uterine contractions continue, but the cervix now allows the gradual propulsion of the fetus through the birth canal. This induces crushing mechanical pressures and explosive discharges of energy, pains, and often a high degree of anoxia and suffocation. This highly uncomfortable and life-threatening situation also generates intense anxiety.

In this stage various dangerous complications may also develop. The umbilical cord can be squeezed between the head and the pelvic opening or be twisted around the neck. The placenta can detach during the delivery or actually obstruct the way out (placenta praevia). In some instances, the fetus can inhale various forms of biological material that it encounters in the final stages of this process, including its own feces (meconium), which further intensifies the feelings of suffocation. The problems in this stage can be so extreme that they require instrumental intervention, such as the use of forceps, suction cup, or even emergency Cesarean section.

BPM III is an extremely rich and complex experiential pattern. Besides the memory imprint of the fetus' struggle in the birth canal, it can be accompanied by a wide variety of symbolic images drawn from history, technology, biology, forces of nature, or mythology. The most important of these themes are an atmosphere of titanic fight, aggressive and sadomasochistic sequences, experiences of deviant sexuality, demonic episodes, scatological excretions, and encounter with fire (pyrocatharsis). Some of these aspects of BPM III can be meaningfully related to certain anatomical, physiological, and biochemical processes of the corresponding stage of birth. Yet some of the most astonishing symbolic images seem to have no direct connection with the memories of biological birth, but rather connected to them through experiential logic.

The titanic aspect of BPM III is quite understandable in view of the enormity of the forces operating in the final stage of childbirth—powerful contractions of the uterus compressing the fetus, whose head is wedged into the narrow pelvic opening with pressures releasing in powerful discharges. In the symbolic images

Experience of bonding and sexual arrousal, painting from a high dose LSD session by Stan Grof

Experience of a wild carnival scene during transition from BPM III to BPM IV,
painting from a high dose LSD session by Stan Grof

we can see raging elements of nature, such as volcanoes, electric storms, earth-
quakes, tidal waves, or tornadoes. We can also experience scenes of technological
devices using enormous energy such as tanks, rockets, spaceships, lasers, electric
power plants, or even thermonuclear reactors and atomic bombs. The titanic experiences of BPM III may also include battles of gigantic proportions, such as the
cosmic battle between the forces of Light and Darkness.

The aggressive and sadomasochistic aspects of this matrix reflect the biological fury of the organism whose survival is threatened by suffocation and
pain, as well as the introjected destructive onslaught of the uterine contractions.
Experiencing BPM III, we can encounter images of fetuses together with symbolic
scenes such as violent murders and suicides, massacres of various kinds, or bloody
wars and revolutions.

The experiential logic of the sexual aspect of the death-rebirth process is not as immediately obvious. It seems that the human organism has an inherent physiological mechanism that translates inhuman suffering, and particularly suffocation, into a strange kind of sexual arousal of a pornographic or deviant nature, and eventually into ecstatic rapture.

When the experience of BPM III comes closer to resolution, it becomes less violent and disturbing. The prevailing atmosphere is that of extreme passion and driving energy of intoxicating intensity. The imagery tends to portray exciting conquests of new territories, hunting behavior of wild animals, extreme sports, and adventures in amusement parks. These experiences are clearly related to activities that involve an "adrenaline rush"—parachuting, bungee jumping, car racing, acrobatic diving, dangerous stunts, or circus performances. Just before the experience of psychospiritual rebirth, it is also common to encounter the element of fire. The fire seems to radically destroy whatever is corrupted in us and prepare us for spiritual rebirth. Though none of the fantastic symbolic images and scenes of BPM III are based directly on the memory of biological birth, they share the intense excitement, passion, and fear aroused during delivery. I termed the type of ecstasy associated with BPM III *volcanic* or *Dionysian* ecstasy.

The fourth perinatal matrix (BPM IV)—the *Death-Rebirth Experience*—is related to the third clinical stage of delivery. Here we conclude the difficult process of propulsion through the birth canal, achieve explosive liberation, and emerge into the light. This experience also often coincides with dramatic scientific, artistic, political, and religious breakthroughs; I coined this outburst of creativity the Promethean type of ecstasy. BPM IV often portrays concrete and realistic memories of various specific aspects of the final stages of birth. These can include the experience of anesthesia, pressure of the forceps, the sensations associated with various obstetric maneuvers or postnatal interventions, washing and cleaning of the newborn, and bonding with the mother.

Reliving biological birth is not a simple replay of the original biological event, but a profound psychospiritual death and rebirth. The question arises: "Why not just rebirth—where does the element of death come from?" In this process we can actually encounter death in three different ways. First, depending on how difficult the passage through the birth canal is, the fetus can come close to death or even die and need to be resuscitated. Second, when the umbilical cord is cut, the body of the fetus undergoes a radical anatomical and physiological transformation. It inflates its lungs and begins to breathe, eat, urinate, and defecate. During the pregnancy these functions were all taken care of by the mother's body. At this

Experience of Maha Kali, surrendering as a Male
to the Feminine, painting from a high dose LSD session
by Stan Grof

time, the newborn essentially dies and ceases to exist as an aquatic organism and becomes an air-breathing human being.

You said that the fetus experiences three deaths? Is the third death the ego death? Could you explain what, for you, is the ego that dies during the experience of the ego death?

Yes it is the ego that dies but not the part of the ego that Freud defined as *"the function that is able to perceive objective reality and respond to it adequately"*—a necessary function, which we develop in childhood. The part of the ego that dies during ego death is that which is formed in response to the intense emotional and physical suffering in labor. The fetus is completely confined during the delivery by the birth canal and has no way of expressing the extreme emotions and physical sensations generated during this suffering. The memory of birth remains psychologically undigested and unassimilated. In a sense, we were born anatomically but

Final stage of death and rebirth, peacock heaven
of the Great Mother Goddess, painting from a high dose
LSD session by Stan Grof

have not completed this process emotionally. The ego death that precedes rebirth is the death of our old concepts of who we are and what the world is like; these concepts were forged by the traumatic imprint of birth. As we clear these old programs from the unconscious, they dissolve and lose their emotional charge, essentially "dying."

We have identified with these old programs to such an extent that when the unauthentic ego is seriously threatened, it feels like the end of our existence, or even the end of the whole world. As frightening as this process is, it is actually very healing and transformative. Paradoxically, while only a small step separates us from an experience of radical liberation, we have a sense of all-pervading anxiety and impending catastrophe of enormous proportions. What actually dies in this process is the false ego that—up to this point in our life—we have mistaken for our true Self. As we lose all the reference points we know, we have no idea what is on the other side, or even if there is anything there at all. This fear tends

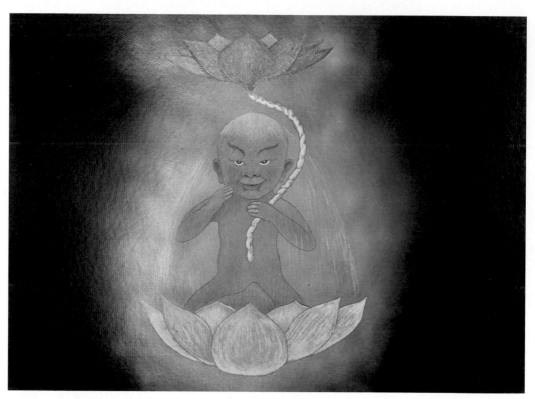

The Divine Child, Buddha Baby, painting from a high dose LSD session by Stan Grof

to create an enormous resistance to continue and complete the experience. As a result, without appropriate guidance, many people can remain psychologically stuck in this problematic territory.

When we, at this important juncture, overcome the metaphysical fear and decide to let go, we experience total annihilation on all imaginable levels: physical destruction, emotional disaster, intellectual and philosophical defeat, ultimate moral degradation, and spiritual damnation. During this experience, all reference points, everything that is important and meaningful in life, seem to be mercilessly destroyed. Immediately following the experience of total annihilation—hitting "cosmic bottom"—we are overwhelmed by visions of white or golden light of supernatural radiance and exquisite beauty that is numinous and Divine. Having survived what seemed like an experience of total annihilation and the apocalyptic end of everything, we are blessed only seconds later with fantastic displays of magnificent rainbow spectra, peacock designs, celestial scenes, and visions of mythological beings bathed in Divine Light.

The discovery of the perinatal matrices was an important step toward the new expanded cartography of the psyche. You also tried to explain in some of your early books how the integration of the BPMs can help to resolve many important problems in psychiatry. Can you describe a few of these examples?

When I assembled enough evidence that the memories of the biological birth are recorded in the unconscious, I was surprised that this fact, which seemed so obvious, had not yet been accepted by mainstream academicians and clinicians. The newborn child's brain is highly developed and should be able to register the birth process—a stressful situation that lasts many hours or even days and often borders on death. I wrote in my books and articles that psychiatry cannot explain many important facts because it does not accept the memory of the birth trauma and the perinatal matrices. For example, the manner and intensity of human violence cannot be explained by contemporary biology or psychiatry. Until his death, Freud also unsuccessfully struggled to solve the puzzle of sadomasochism. He could not understand the strange fusion of the basic biological instincts—sexuality and aggression. He also did not well explain some of the other sexual variations, aberrations, and perversions—Richard von Krafft-Ebing's *Psychopathia sexualis.*

Freud tried to interpret these sexual disorders as arising from the postnatal level of the psyche, by libidinal fixations on the erogenous zones and the blocking of libido by the superego. However, all these phenomena appear much more logical if we relate them to BPM II and BPM III. Pain and suffocation generate an intense driving energy, which is very similar to the sexual drive (libido). This sexual energy is mixed during birth with strong feelings of aggression; this drive is oriented both inward (the force of the uterine contractions) and outward (the reaction to the pain and fear of death). Thus in BPM III, sexuality, aggression, and contact with biological materials (amniotic fluid, blood, urine, meconium, feces, and vaginal secretions) play an important role in sexual aberrations and criminal sexuality, including rape and sexual murder.

The exploration of the perinatal matrices in LSD therapy greatly deepens and expands the model envisioned by Freudian psychoanalysis. Psychedelic therapy and holotropic breathwork showed that Freud and his early pioneers were on the right track with their efforts to understand the origin of emotional and psychosomatic disorders such as conversion hysteria and anxiety hysteria (phobias), obsessive compulsive neurosis, psychogenic asthma, depression, suicides, sexual deviations, and others. Unfortunately, their ineffective methods—verbal psychotherapy, free associations, work with transference neurosis, avoidance of physical contact, strategic silence, and others—seemed to work on the postnatal level yet did not reach to the most important roots of the patients' problems. The superficial and truncated interpretations of psychoanalysis are unconvincing and often bizarre and ridiculous, for example, when Freud tried to explain suicide as killing the introjected breast of the bad mother.

Many mainstream therapists essentially gave up on investigating the psychodynamic roots of emotional problems and etiological diagnoses, as the "neo-Kraepelinian" approach that emerged limited itself to the description of symptoms, exemplified in the *Diagnostic and Statistical Manual of Mental Disorders* (DSM). However, the powerful expressive therapies that can reach to the perinatal matrices (and even deeper to transpersonal experiences) offer much more logical and satisfactory etiological explanations of emotional disorders. The understanding and activation of the perinatal matrices (BPM II and III) in therapy offer much more convincing explanations and treatment for conditions such as phobias, inhibited and agitated depression, non-violent and violent suicide, and psychosomatic pain. Working with perinatal and transpersonal experiences is also instrumental in successfully treating rapid-onset psychogenic psychoses, for which we coined the term "spiritual emergency."

Contemporary psychiatry has no satisfactory explanation for most ritual, spiritual, and religious experiences, activities and events that are meaningful for most of the people on our planet. Psychiatrists see religious phenomena as superstition, primitive magical thinking, or delusions and hallucinations of borderline or schizophrenic individuals.

When it was discovered and confirmed that we carry in our unconscious the memories of biological birth, these discoveries became highly significant for the study of theology and comparative religion. I was very excited to discover that the four perinatal matrices match the range of possible abodes of the soul described in many religions. Undisturbed experiences of BPM I—existence beyond space and time, blissful and tranquil with a mystical or ecstatic feeling—share the quality of the various heavens and paradises in religions around the world and from all time periods. The problematic BPM I experiences of disturbances of intrauterine life, a prenatal environment with toxic amniotic fluid, have a parallel in the underworld rivers—dirty, muddy, and polluted, and flowing toward death, such as the Greek Styx or Mayan Xibalba. The transition from BPM I to BPM II resembles the Expulsion from Eden or Paradise Lost as described by John Milton.

The extreme emotional and physical suffering, sense of no exit, hopelessness, helplessness, and suffocating oppression of BPM II has all the essential qualities of hell. St. John of the Cross described the shattering experience of terrifying darkness and utter despair, referring to it as the Dark Night of the Soul; and in

Dante Alighieri holding a copy of the *Divine Comedy* next to the entrance to hell, the seven terraces of Mount Purgatory, and the city of Florence with the spheres of Heaven above

her autobiography, St. Teresa of Avila described hell as a suffocating place of unendurable torments, where she was cramped in a small hole. BPM III brings intense emotional and somatic suffering, and intolerable burning heat. However, it is not a hopeless situation; there is a sense of finite suffering and the possibility of escape to a better situation, of purging fire and cleansing. These experiences have the qualities of purgatory. Several of my patients in LSD sessions also identified, in their BPM III experiences, with Hindu and Christian ascetics and medieval flagellants. In psychedelic sessions many people see during their BPM IV experiences radiant white, blue, or golden light; rainbow arcs; and peacock feathers. They can experience psychospiritual death and rebirth, the ascent to Heaven, Divine Epiphany, the *hieros gamos* or sacred marriage, or visions of Great Mother Goddesses or God. These visions appear in forms described in various religions around the world.

The perinatal matrices also provide fascinating insight into shamanism. The onset of BPM II is similar to the beginning of the shamanic initiation. The novice shaman undergoes a visionary journey, descends into the underworld, is attacked by evil spirits, and experiences extreme emotional and physical suffering. He or she is subjected to severe ordeals, is annihilated, dismembered, and then reborn. From there he or she undergoes a magical journey to the supernal realm, following a track similar to the transition from BPM III to IV. During the initiatory journey, the novice often heals him or herself from various diseases and learns how to heal others.

Rose of Angels in Dante's *Divine Comedy* by Gustave Dore

After successful integration of this inner journey, the shaman often then becomes a healer, psychopomp, artist, or leader of their tribe.

Over the years, many of my psychedelic clients and participants in holotropic breathwork experienced classic episodes of shamanic initiation. These were often combined with perinatal and childbirth imagery. Additional examples of the manifestation of perinatal matrices are the rites of passage, rituals that were performed in most pre-industrial countries of the world during the time of important biological or social transitions. My patients and trainees in psychedelic and holotropic breathwork sessions experienced sequences similar to the rites of Australian Aboriginal, African, Native American, and Indian tribes. Joseph Campbell discovered that the three stages of rites of passage are identical with the perinatal matrices II–IV: Separation (BPM II), Initiation or Transformation (BPM III), and Return (BPM IV).

These discoveries were exciting and I know that you were initially surprised and thrilled how many new areas in psychiatry opened up. But you also found some serious challenges in your theory that took you far beyond birth and the perinatal matrices.

Initiation ritual at the Mandan Okipa Festival of the Plain Indians

It is true that I was very excited to be able to confirm the existence of birth memories and of the perinatal matrices, yet that also brought further difficult problems. In our LSD sessions, we were not only able to experience the fetal memories through the stages of BPM I, II, and III. Besides the fetal and childbirth scenes, the BPMs often feature complex symbolic scenes that follow experiential logic, as we have seen. In the case of hell and purgatory in BPM II and III, the emotions, pains, pressures, and choking could be explained as part of the fetal memories, but not the horrifying devils with pitchforks and nooses torturing sinners or burning them by flames of fire. The same were panoramas of epic wars and revolutions or Witches Sabbath during BPM III. The BPM I and IV sequences featured glorious visions of the universe, deities in golden light, heavens and paradises of various cultures, ecstatic ocean lifeforms, and beautiful dancing Polynesians on unspoiled islands. These could not be explained simply as birth memories.

It was even more remarkable that my clients in their LSD sessions saw visions at the time of the transition from BPM III to IV of mythological death-rebirth deities from different cultures and historical periods, such as the Sumerian Inanna, Egyptian Isis and Osiris, Greek Persephone and Dionysus, Nordic Wotan,

Joseph Campbell

Hawaiian Pele, and Aztec Quetzalcoatl. Several of my Czech and American clients experienced these deities with unusual details although they had not previously been familiar with them. On occasion we had to consult special academic sources to confirm the descriptions in their session reports and paintings.

When I immigrated to the U.S. and needed mythological consultation about my psychedelic patients or holotropic breathwork participants, I called my brilliant friend Joseph Campbell, who was a "walking mythological lexicon." In most cases, he was able to identify the deities—even obscure ones—from the people's mandalas and verbal descriptions. Once I told Joe about an LSD patient whom I had treated in Prague for thanatophobia. In one of his sessions, he encountered a Terrible Pig Goddess sitting in front of a large entrance into the underworld. This deity demanded that my patient draw a specific geometrical pattern; without it, she would not allow him to pass into the Beyond. I tried to understand what this mysterious story was about, but my efforts were in vain. Joe was excited and fascinated; he said promptly: "This was the Polynesian Goddess of Death and Night of the Malekulan culture from New Guinea. The Malekulans had to practice during their lives to draw a very complex geometrical pattern, because without it their Goddess would not let them pass after their death to the Beyond.

There now exists much support for the existence of memories of birth. Those of us who experienced psychedelic and holotropic breathwork sessions often witnessed participants who relived specific birth memories that could often then be confirmed. But as you said, much of the images that we see in perinatal

matrices cannot be explained from birth memories. The fetus could not have seen all the elements that people often experience during BPM I, II, and III sessions. The same is true of the symbolic visions and mythological personages and sceneries that appeared in perinatal matrices; they have to come from a different source than the birth memories.

Yes, as we have seen, the perinatal matrices consist of fetal images and also characteristic mythological and symbolic components that follow experiential logic. But I wondered, what was the mysterious source of these symbolic images if not from the birth memories? I later kept seeing the same kind of symbolic experiences after the fetal/childbirth experiences disappeared from some of my clients' and from my own sessions. I have also seen that the same images can emerge in the sessions of people who had been born by elective Caesarean section. I then began to refer to as perinatal experiences only those that included fetal images, and I created a new category of experiences, coining for them the term "transpersonal." Several months ago, a Canadian friend and psychiatrist wrote me an email. He was surprised because one of his patients had a high dose of psilocybin and experienced a "classic BPM III experience," although he had been born by elective Caesarean section. We will return to this problem later in connection with archetypal astrology.

The completion of one's facing and processing the perinatal layer of the psyche does not end the exploration of the deep unconscious. People who have no more fetal experiences in their psychedelic sessions can encounter a vast array of transpersonal experiences. Regression can continue to prenatal life, to embryogenesis, and even to the experience of conception with the fusion of spermatozoid and ovum. I have seen in LSD sessions many powerful experiences of ancestral, racial, karmic, and phylogenetic consciousness, with experiential identification continuing backward along Darwin's evolutionary tree. In psychedelic sessions it is possible to experience the consciousness of plankton in the ocean, bacteria, and even viruses.

Preceding the experience of conception, the only possible material substrates remaining for memory are the nuclei of the spermatozoids and ova, chromosomes, and DNA. Some scientists, who had experienced LSD, tried to talk about DNA consciousness in an effort to save the materialistic philosophy. But even the far-fetched idea that DNA could carry all the experiences from the distant past that emerge in LSD sessions runs into serious problems. To encounter in LSD sessions an authentic experiential identification with certain animals, for example, a chimpanzee or silverback gorilla, the DNA would have to flow back and then forward to the side branches of the evolutionary tree. Thus, from at least as deeply

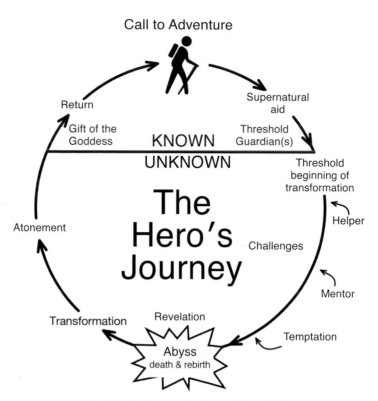

The Hero's Journey by Joseph Campbell

as the perinatal matrices, we have to abandon the idea of material substrates for memory to understand what is happening in psychedelic sessions. We need a source that transcends material substrates, such as Rupert Sheldrake's morpho-genetic fields, Ervin Laszlo's Akashic holofield, or Alfred North Whitehead's Process Philosophy.

Joseph Campbell, motivated by C. G. Jung, collected myths from all over the world and many historical periods. Campbell was astonished when he found similar myths and stories across all the continents, countries, cultures, and even isolated tribes. These myths featured gods and goddesses, demigods, and legendary heroes who experienced death and rebirth. In many places, these myths inspired the ancient mystery religions of death and rebirth. Joe was also surprised to discover that these universal myths followed the pattern found within the basic perinatal matrices. He eventually wrote *The Hero with a Thousand Faces* and later *The Hero's Journey,* outlining his discovery that the same basic story exists in the entire spiritual life of planet Earth, though with myriads of local variations.

These stories have been recounted to children, to young, adult, and old people on every continent; many of them have been passed by mouth for centuries, even for millennia. Joe Campbell recalled this phenomenon of a universal pattern the monomyth; Phil Cousineau later expanded the term to metamonomyth. These similar mythic patterns are ubiquitous yet could not have been explained by sharing via travel by water or land. They appear also in the psychedelic sessions of people who had never previously heard about them.

This phenomenal global archive of myths is available to people who enter holotropic states of consciousness in psychedelic or holotropic sessions, in spiritual crises, and in spiritual practice. C. G. Jung confirmed that elements of these myths emerge from the collective unconscious in dreams, in the reports of psychiatric patients, in moments of artistic inspiration, even in individuals who have never known about them. Further, the myths are not spread at random over the globe. They are distributed like an intelligent taxonomist from the center of the continents to the periphery. In a scheme sketched by Marie-Louise von Franz, the ramification and spread of cultural myths looks like an image of budding yeast.

My journey to understanding LSD and other holotropic states of consciousness resembled an exciting and challenging treasure hunt. Each finding on the way

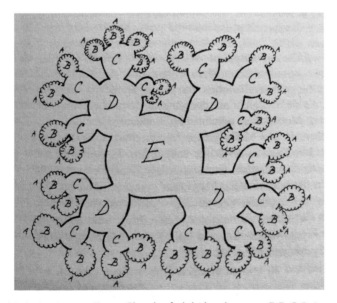

Marie-Louise von Franz: Sketch of global archetypes: E-D-C-B-A
(the whole Earth E, continents D, lands C, regions B, tribes A)

pointed to the next clue; what seemed to be an answer soon opened out into another question. The last clue, which is so far the most unexpected and promising, was a rediscovery from Greek philosophy and cosmology: the understanding of the archetypal forms and of archetypal astrology. This was such an important step that I refer to archetypal astrology as "the Rosetta Stone of consciousness research."

How did you make the transition in your research from perinatal matrices, transpersonal experiences, and mythology to archetypes and astrology?

The last major contribution to my understanding of LSD and the expanded cartography of the psyche came in 1973 when I moved to the Esalen Institute in Big Sur, California, and began to collaborate with Richard Tarnas. Rick came to Esalen to work with me on his Ph.D. dissertation on LSD psychotherapy. Arne Trettevik, a participant in one of our month-long workshops, who was an experienced astrologer, suggested that we should learn astrology and use it to illuminate our psychedelic work. After some hesitation, we agreed to explore this avenue and Arne taught us how to compute and draw natal charts.

Rick was working at Esalen as a night guard and spent much time watching the stunning star-spangled night sky above the Pacific Ocean. During the daytimes when he worked in the guard shack, as Esalen residents and workshop participants found out that he was interested in astrology, they lined up to get readings from him. Many of the life adventures and stories they shared with him for feedback were from holotropic breathwork sessions, Gestalt practice, spiritual emergency experiences, and some from psychedelic sessions. Rick was also working in his free time on his dissertation and we were enjoying many discussions about, among other things, the COEX systems and perinatal matrices.

We discovered to our astonishment and surprise that the four BPMs had a dramatic resemblance to passages from a typical astrological handbook on the meanings associated with the four outermost planets: BPM I with Neptune, BPM II with Saturn, BPM III with Pluto, and BPM IV with Uranus. This seemed to us to be an incredible synchronicity, since I extrapolated the existence of the BPMs from observing thousands of my patients' sessions, long before knowing anything about astrology. After a short period came another astonishing observation—Rick found that the four BPMs play important roles in the sessions of people at the time when the corresponding planets are activated in their charts by transit. This unexpected liaison between LSD experiences and the planetary archetypes threw light on previously unexplainable problems.

Rick Tarnas at Esalen 1986

What is your understanding of archetypes, the planets as astronomical bodies, and their role in psychedelic experiences?

Archetypes are cosmic primordial patterns and governing principles; they are universals that function as templates for the particulars of the material world. The original Greek word means "first-molded" (from ἀρχή, meaning "beginning" or "origin" and τύπος, meaning "pattern," "model," or "type"). Archetypes are abstract universal matrices that are themselves transphenomenal but that can manifest in many different forms and on many different levels of reality.

Rick Tarnas describes in his 2006 book, *Cosmos and Psyche: Intimations of a New World View,* three broad understandings and perspectives on the archetypes. They can be perceived as:

1. Mythological principles (in Homer's epics, the Greek tragedies, and world mythology)
2. Philosophical principles (in the philosophy of Socrates, Plato, and Aristotle)
3. Psychological principles (in the psychology of C. G. Jung).

In his magnum opus Rick explored over thirty years of historical research in which he correlated planetary aspects and transits with the lifework of famous individuals and important events in science, technology, art, politics, philosophy, and spirituality. Besides confirming persuasive and consistent correlations in these areas, he was able to demonstrate, through many examples, that planetary archetypes have multivalent meanings, while at the same time remaining true to their essential thematic nature. Archetypes have no specific concrete form in and of themselves but can be expressed in many of their multivalent potentialities. Which of the many possible manifestations of the planetary archetypes will emerge at any given time seems to be based on factors such as the relationship people have with their own psyches, whether they have access to deep processing, their age and stage of life, the cultural context, and, as Rick suggests, perhaps unmeasurables such as karma and grace.

In holotropic states of consciousness, we can sometimes receive insights into the multivalence of the archetypes, as if they were manifesting as holographic images. I described in *The Way of the Psychonaut II* an example of holographic psychedelic experiences in one of my own sessions. In it I seemed to be viewing a kind of cosmic theater in which the archetypes were featured as actors in the great Cosmic Game (*lila*). There was Maya, the mysterious ethereal principle symbolizing the world illusion; Anima, embodying the eternal Female; a Mars-like personification of war and aggression; the Lovers, representing all the sexual dramas and romances throughout the ages; the royal figure of the Ruler; the withdrawn Hermit; the elusive Trickster; and many others.

Returning to our discussion of the four outer planetary archetypes and their corresponding BPMs, we can begin with Neptune (BPM I): This multivalent, multileveled archetype represents the dissolution of boundaries between the human individual and other people, nature, the entire universe, and God. It manifests as experiences of mystical union and cosmic consciousness; the imaginal world, spiritual realms, idealistic dreams and aspirations; physical and psychosomatic healing; spiritual longing, heightened intuition, ESP, and creative imagination; the element water in the rivers, lakes, and oceans of the world, bodily fluids, and the amniotic environment of the womb. The shadow side of Neptune can take the form of flights into fantasy, delusion, illusion, self-deception, psychotic distortions of reality, loss of individuality, confusion, and disorientation; alcoholism and drug addiction; and entrapment in the small "r" reality or world of samsara.

Saturn (BPM II). This archetypal complex typically marks critical developmental periods in human life; times of hard labor, difficulties, and challenges; restriction, limitation, scarcity, deficit; oppression, repression, depression, feelings of inferiority and guilt; impermanence, aging, death, the ending of things; difficult personal trials and tribulations; but also the forging of enduring structures, stability that leads to important completions, tradition, and faithfulness in relationships or marriage.

Pluto (BPM III) is an unusually rich and multivalent archetype. It represents the primordial energies of the cosmos, nature, and human society; the energies of destruction and creation; biological processes of birth, sex, and death, instinctual forces in the body and psyche (the Freudian id); psychospiritual death and rebirth, transformation, and regeneration; the underworld (whether urban, social, psychological, mythological, moral, or sexual).

Uranus (BPM IV). This archetype represents the principle of sudden surprises and dramatic change; rebellion against the status quo, revolutionary activity, impulses toward liberation and individualism; spiritual awakening, emotional and intellectual breakthroughs; collapse of established structures; revolutionary insight, creative genius, and originality, inventions and technology, particularly related to electricity, aviation, and space travel. The shadow side of the Uranus archetype includes anarchy, unfruitful eccentricity, and indiscriminate acting out against laws and limitations of any kind. Ouranos was the Greek god of the sky and heavens. Rick Tarnas has demonstrated, however, that the fuller archetypal meaning of Uranus can be understood through its association with the Greek mythic figure Prometheus, the rebellious trickster and liberator (see his book *Prometheus the Awakener*).

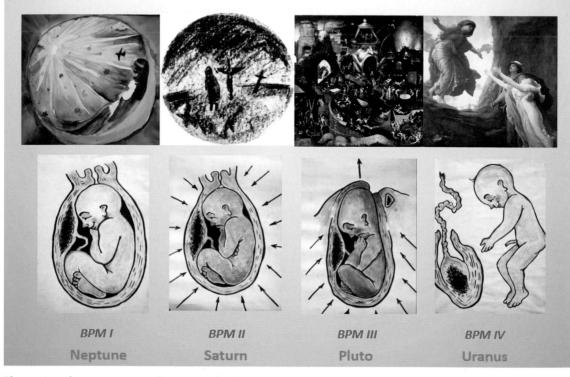

The perinatal sequence according to Grof and Tarnas. BPM I: *In the Lap of the Goddess* by Silvina Heath from a holotropic breathwork session during a transit of Neptune conjunct her natal Moon. BPM II: *Landscape of Everlasting Pain* by Tauno Leinonen from a holotropic breathwork session during a transit of Saturn square his natal Sun. BPM III: *Christ in Limbo* by a follower of Hieronymus Bosch. BPM IV: *The Return of Persephone* by Frederic Leighton during an almost certain transit of Uranus square his natal Moon, and with a natal aspect of Moon opposition Uranus. With special thanks to the artists. Slide by Renn Butler.

The multivalent nature of planetary archetypes helps to explain the symbolic logic of the images that appear with each of the perinatal matrices. Each matrix portrays the fetus in a specific stage of childbirth, but it also includes a number of people, animals, scenes from nature, and situations that contain the same emotions and physical sensations as the essential quality of that BPM. For example, the undisturbed BPM I experiences include the blissful fetus in the amniotic womb; symbolic images that accompany it include the magnificent star-filled sky, the peaceful existence of aquatic lifeforms in the ocean, unspoiled Polynesian islands, sunrises by the seashore, or waterfalls. These are all manifestations of the Neptune archetype and we will usually find that people who experience these BPM I elements in their sessions have positive Neptune transits occurring at the time of their sessions.

As we have seen, the images in the BPMs cannot be explained as memories of biological birth. In LSD sessions we can often see the fetal body inside the mother's belly and uterus, as well as these other symbolic scenes that are connected by experiential or symbolic logic. Both the fetal elements and the corresponding symbolic scenes are ultimately creations of the multivalent planetary archetypes. In this new understanding, the BPMs are concentrated manifestations of the planetary archetypes Neptune, Saturn, Pluto, and Uranus, which will then be further inflected by the additional planetary archetypes involved by transit.

The mythological embodiments of the planetary archetypes will also tend to manifest along with the appropriate perinatal matrices. For example, in BPM I experiences, we might have visions of Bodhisattva, Amita Buddha, Maya, lila, Narcissus; in BPM II: Kronos, the Grim Reaper, personages of the Greek underworld such as Sisyphus, Tantalus, Ixion, Hades and Persephone, or the pre-Columbian death gods Cizin and Mictlantecuhtli; in BPM III: Pluto, Dionysus, Osiris, Kali, Shiva, Rangda, Pele, Quetzalcoatl; and in BPM IV: Prometheus, Helios, the Egyptian god Ra, Ahura Mazda, Barong, or Great Mother Goddesses such as Isis, Demeter, Aphrodite, the Virgin Mary, Laxmi, Sarasvati, or Yamaya.

Many people see astrology as the gold standard of superstition. They do not take astrology seriously, because it seems to them outrageous and ridiculous to imagine that rocks in the sky could have anything to do with historical events, creative talents, emotions, or relations between people. And yet Rick Tarnas and you claim that archetypal astrology can predict in an archetypal-thematic way the content of experiences in psychedelic sessions. How can you explain how intelligent people could believe in astrology?

Rick Tarnas and Stan Grof in Big Sur, filming *The Changing of the Gods* in 2015.

The traditional objections against astrology come from the realm of physics and astronomy, disciplines that are based on the worldview of mechanistic materialism. Astrology does not make sense as long as we think that astrologers are attempting to explain correlations arising from physical forces, such as gravitation, electromagnetic fields, radioactivity, cosmic rays, and so on. During a discussion with Carl Sagan, the famous American astronomer and adversary of astrology, he told me: "Astrology is hogwash; as I am standing here, I have more gravitational influence on you than does Pluto." He clearly thought in terms of mass, distance, gravitational forces, and other physical terms, an approach that completely misses the modern understanding of astrology. Critics of astrology like Carl Sagan do not realize that astrologers are using a sophisticated paradigm that assumes a synchronistic relationship between the planets and archetypes, the human psyche, and external events. To understand astrology, we must learn to think in a radically different paradigm and in synchronistic terms.

We have to understand that the universe was created by an unimaginable intelligence. The primordial governing principles or cosmic forces within this intelligence are the archetypes. These creative principles are somehow coordinated with the movements of the planets as they form angular patterns with each other. The planets are not causing events in the world or human experiences; they simply indicate, in a synchronistic way, what the state of the archetypal realm is at any given time.

We can illustrate the relation between the angular alignments of the planets and the activation of archetypal principles in human experience with a simple example. When I look at my watch, which has the correct time, and it shows that it is seven o'clock, I can infer that all the watches and clocks in the same time zone, which also have the correct time, will show that it is also seven o'clock. I can further assume with reasonable certainty that if I turn on the TV, I will be able to see the seven o'clock news or that my arrival will be expected at the restaurant where I had made a seven o'clock reservation. This naturally does not mean that my watch has a direct influence on other watches and clocks in the environment, that it causes TV news, or interacts with the awareness of the restaurant personnel. All these events are simply synchronized in relation to astronomical time, a hidden dimension that is operating "behind the scenes" and cannot be directly perceived. Since the planets are visible, they can be used to infer what is happening in the world of the archetypes. Their angular relationship to the positions of the planets in our natal chart, by transit, indicates how the corresponding archetypal dynamics might manifest in our personal life—including in a psychedelic session.

Stan Grof at the ITA conference in Prague 2017

Can you suggest how archetypal astrology might help me in psychedelic therapy—to help clarify what I experienced in my sessions in the past, preparing for a session now, or choosing the best dates for sessions in the future?

We have so far talked about the four major planetary archetypes and their multivalent manifestations. There are ten major bodies in the solar system that archetypal astrologers look at, including the Sun and Moon, which are in a constant dynamic interplay as they form ongoing alignments with each other. The combinations and influences of the planets on each other also resemble Wagner's Leitmotifs. When we take LSD, we tune into the field of the archetypes that are currently engaged by transit. The emerging experiences that embody the character of this archetypal field can come from any layer of the unconscious: postnatal, perinatal, or transpersonal (karmic, historical, phylogenetic, mythological, and others). The depth and intensity of these experiences will then depend on the dosage used, the set and setting, the previous number of introspective experiences, the level of spiritual practice, the quality of trust with the sitters or guides, and the planetary transits in effect.

The range of possible expressions and combinations of the multivalent archetypes engaged by transits is large and allows great creativity and even cosmic humor in the divine play. It is also interesting how COEX systems are involved in archetypal-astrological manifestations—i.e., the major aspects in a person's chart will tend to correspond to important COEX systems in their psyches. Furthermore, the activation of these natal aspects by transit will then reveal when those COEX systems are most likely to surface into consciousness for deep processing and resolution. Astrology can thus be used to illuminate experiences in the past, present, or future. However, the type of predictions we can legitimately make will be of an archetypal rather than a concrete, specific nature—we always have to allow for the full range, multivalence, and multileveled nature of the planetary archetypes.

Now that you have explored the different periods and stages of your LSD research, from pharmacological to archetypal, what is your present understanding of this remarkable substance?

The sixty-five years during which I have been investigating LSD and other psychedelics have been a journey of remarkable adventures of discovery and self-discovery. Responding to the observations of LSD experiences, it was necessary to make some radical revisions and additions to the model used in psychiatry and psychology. The cartography of the psyche had to be vastly expanded and deepened with the inclusion of two large additional domains, the perinatal and the transpersonal; the latter realm overlaps significantly with Jung's idea of the collective unconscious. This new cartography in psychiatry can explain much of what the old psychiatry could not do—for example, the nature and intensity of human violence, most emotional and psychosomatic disorders, and the ritual, spiritual, and religious life of humanity (shamanism, rites of passage, the ancient mysteries of death and rebirth, and practices and experiences of the great religions).

Psychedelics have shown us that the mechanistic materialistic worldview that we have inherited from the seventeenth century is seriously outdated and needs to be replaced by a post-materialistic philosophy and cosmology that can account for the observations of psychedelic therapy and bridge the gaping chasm between science and religion. If psychiatry and psychology can integrate into their understanding the perinatal and transpersonal domains of the psyche, work directly with holotropic states of consciousness, and learn to trust the inner healing intelligence of the client's own psyche, it would greatly improve the effectiveness of therapy and healing in these fields. I hope that in the future we will have facilities in which experienced therapists and sitters will use psychedelics and other holotropic states of consciousness in a deep and responsible way, with guidance from archetypal astrology.

I have observed that my LSD patients and trainees in holotropic breathwork, who experienced an entire series of sessions, not only improved their emotional condition and overall well-being, but also independently developed a similar positive worldview, system of values, and life philosophy. They showed an increase in racial, sexual, political, and religious tolerance and replaced competitiveness as a life strategy with one of synergy and cooperation. They automatically developed a love of nature, great ecological sensitivity, and a feeling of belonging to humanity and sense of planetary citizenship. Another important quality has been a strong rejection of violence as an acceptable means of solving conflicts. Perhaps most surprising was the emergence, in many of my clients and trainees, of spirituality of a mystical nature, one that tends to be nonsectarian, nondenominational, universal, all-inclusive, and all-encompassing. I have seen this kind of transformation emerge in many hundreds of people. If it were possible to achieve this change in large numbers of people, humanity would have a better chance to survive the many crises that are ahead of us.

Thank you so much, Stan, for this interview and for everything you have brought to humanity with your dedicated research in holotropic states of consciousness and psychedelics over this long period of your life! Happy Birthday and many more wonderful years of life to come!

Stan and Brigitte Grof celebrating Stan's birthday at their home in Germany

Birthday
Greetings

Chris and Christina Bache

Dear Stan,

When one person changes another person's life as deeply as you have changed mine, one can't help but suspect a destiny planted at the soul level before our earthly lives began. I read *Realms of the Human Unconscious* in 1978, just as I was beginning my academic career, and suddenly there you were, opening doors and setting my mind on fire. In that first encounter you changed the landscape of my life, and I began my own psychedelic journey. Since that time, practically everything I have written has been in dialogue with your groundbreaking work.

It was only years later that we met in person, and I felt your personal warmth and massive presence. I remember watching you move around the room at a large holotropic breathwork gathering at the Omega Institute in 1985, kneeling beside people and helping them release pains they had been holding all their lives. What an extraordinary healer you are.

Thank you for bringing me into your community of explorers, for the invitations you extended to me to present at the large ITA conferences and smaller meetings here and there. Among these, the gathering at Esalen in 2000 to explore the broader implications of your work stands out in my mind. Such extraordinary people. Little did I know that I would later marry one of them, Christina Hardy, who, as program coordinator of PCC, had handled the logistics of our meeting. Such is the wonder of the weave that connects us.

By pushing the boundaries of human experience, Stan, you have created a new clearing in the history of Western thought, seeded a new psychedelic lineage, and begun a transmission of new insights into our universe. Your influence will continue to unfold for generations.

I close with words I wrote to you as I was finishing *Dark Night, Early Dawn* but did not send you at the time. I send them to you now with deep gratitude for all the love, healing, and insight you have brought into the world.

Christina joins me in sending you love and blessings on this special birthday.

Chris Bache, Ph.D., professor emeritus in philosophy and religious studies at Youngstown State University, author of LSD and the Mind of the Universe

To Stan

Following your footprints
has been no easy trek.
I would not have had the courage
to go where I have gone
had I not known that you had gone there first
and survived,
You Who Go Before.

And yet
I have struggled with our differences.
Only slowly did I see
that every human being is a unique prism
that bounces light differently.
There is no exploring the Sacred but in this way.

As I awaken in this fellowship
I am ever grateful for the trail you left us,
and what you have shown us of our Mother
through the prism of your being.
Thank you for the vision
of her Beauty,
and Wonder,
and Mystery.

January 27, 1998

Dear Stan,

Happy 90th Birthday! Reading *Realms of the Human Unconscious* changed my life and drew me into my present career, which I love! Thank you.

Robin Carhart-Harris, Ph.D.,
faculty of medicine, Imperial College, London

Dear Stan,

I am wishing all my best wishes for your 90th birthday. I hope that you are well and that you enjoy it. As you know, your many friends and colleagues have always respected you and admired you as a man of wisdom. I believe that you have been wise for many many years! Now that you have reached 90, you have the age that many associate with wisdom, but you had it since you were a young man; now you can rightfully claim both age and wisdom! In the last few decades we have witnessed a revolution in the field of psychedelic therapies. You were and are a pioneer, and because of your work, many people have been helped and healed. Thank you for all that you have done for the field, and for so many who have suffered less thanks to you. May you bask in the warmth and love of your friends and family on this important milestone of your life's journey.

Dennis McKenna, Ph.D.,
ethnopharmacologist, research pharmacognosist, lecturer, and author

S tan is one of the intellectual giants of our time. He has built upon and reshaped the contributions of Freud, Jung, Hofmann, Hillman, and others to provide a new cosmology of consciousness and human potential. Ever since I first met him at Esalen in 1985, having known of him for several years before that, I have been struck by his combination of curiosity and humility. I've experienced Stan as always open for whatever is new and illuminating, whatever will lead to deeper understanding, whatever will catalyze higher consciousness. Stan is a true scientist, a true psychonaut. His curiosity has sculpted in him the modesty of a seeker who knows he does not know and is thus genuinely accessible to seekers everywhere as all of us seek to fathom the mysteries of a cosmos beyond imagination. Stan also embodies joy, born out of the profound love he and Brigitte share. That love has conjured an aliveness, an exuberance, an élan vital that augurs well for many more years of life, love, and exploration.

Jim Garrison, founder and president of Ubiquity University

In Remembrance of Stanislav Grof's 90th Birthday

It is an honor to be included in this collection of remembrances of our friend, the inimitable Stanislav Grof. One of the great good fortunes in my life was having Stan as a teacher, a colleague, and most importantly, a friend. I probably don't need to tell anyone who is reading this book that Stan is undoubtably the greatest psychotherapeutic researcher of psychedelic and other non-ordinary states and, along with Jung perhaps, our preeminent transpersonal theorist. But what I appreciate most about Stan is his kindness and generosity of spirit. Those qualities are not immediately apparent upon meeting him, as Stan possesses a rather imposing presence and air. However, those who have been fortunate enough to venture past this outer veneer have discovered a man of almost inestimable intelligence, wisdom, and warmth.

I wish I could have found an old photo I have somewhere of Stan looking up at a total solar eclipse off the coast of Hawaii. His look of concentration and rapture (experiencing a total eclipse IS an amazing thing) says a lot about this man. The wonderful thing is that it does not take a total eclipse to seize Stan's full attention. He equally loves a good meal, a good joke, and all the other basic experiences that make us human. He especially relishes novelty and intensity, which Whitehead says are the defining characteristics of Life and Spirit. These qualities capture Stan's essence as well as anything that I could say about my dear friend, to whom I send my love and gratitude upon his entering the ninetieth year of this adventure we call life.

John H. Buchanan, Ph.D.,
president of Helios Foundation

Dearest Stan,

It is such a pleasure to participate in the honoring and celebration of your 90th birthday!

My earliest encounter with your work came through *The Human Encounter with Death*. As a young professional woman in her thirties, working in the field of end-of-life care, I was drawn to a public lecture and workshop in Austin, Texas, in 1986. In that first exposure to the depth and breath of your cartography and the field of Transpersonal Psychology, my world was rocked. When you announced that you were looking for thirty students interested in an in-depth, three-year course of study, I leapt at the opportunity!

It has been my good fortune to know you as a teacher, mentor, colleague, traveling companion, and friend for the last thirty-five years. As you know, your work and worldview has informed my life, both personally and professionally, in deep and lasting ways.

I am especially grateful for having had the opportunity to travel the globe as we introduced the underpinnings of Transpersonal Psychology and conducted training in holotropic breathwork—often at potent social/political moments in time in countries like the Czech Republic, Argentina, Chile, Scandinavia, Russia, Ukraine, and China. I continue to be so moved by the possibility of experiencing deep intimacy and connection despite the lack of shared personal history, or even a shared language—and to be reminded again and again that the human experience/the human heart is the same all over the world.

I am wishing you good health, great happiness, and deep peace in the years ahead.

Blessings,
Diane Haug, director of Grof® Legacy Project U.S.

Dear Stan,

What a joy to celebrate your 90th Birthday and your contribution to the world over the past many decades! You have cleared a path for so many of us to find our own way back to the sacred—and to discover our own unique gifts in a magical and conscious universe. My heart is full with the realization that your work is growing ever deeper roots in this time of global transition and, I pray, beginning of the restoration of our alignment with the Earth and the Cosmos. At the personal level, my life holds so much more vitality and joy for having found you, Brigitte, and your work. With the deepest gratitude, I am honored to work with so many others in helping your legacy grow and sharing your contributions with an ever-expanding community of awakening souls.

Much love,
Jay Dufrechou, J.D., Ph.D., educator, lawyer/mediator,
director of Grof® Legacy Training USA

Will Keepin, Cynthia Brix, and Stan Grof

Dearest Stan,

What a great joy and privilege to honor you on this 90th birthday!

It is difficult to conceive the magnitude of profound influence you've had in my life, and in this world—much less to try to find words to express it, which is impossible. In honor of your birthday, let me share just a bit of what you have meant to me.

There are so many rich dimensions to the gifts you have brought into my life, it's hard to fathom. The Grof Breathwork has been such a profound blessing on personal and professional levels—and brought a remarkable gift in working with thousands of clients over the years, and so beautifully deepened and enhanced all the group process trainings, retreats, and programs I have conducted.

The breathwork plus my own psychedelic and ayahuasca journeys and other mystical experiences opened me up to the vast spectrum and majestic depths of human consciousness. Your work and influence on me deeply informed the development of the Gender Equity and Reconciliation work, and taught me to to trust the "collective alchemy" of deep group spiritual transformation. The awakening to archetypal cosmology and astrology have been another major and radical awakening for me, and utterly transformed my entire worldview as a scientist. You literally helped to reset my life and vocation in a whole new, transformative direction and mission—for which I'm forever grateful.

Beyond all this, knowing you personally, and the gift of our long friendship, and your unceasing mentoring and love for me, has been such a remarkable blessing in my life. I cannot thank you enough for all this, Stan.

These words are inadequate to express my love and the deep gratitude in my heart for you. Thank you Stan, and I honor and bless you on this 90th birthday!

My love and gratitude to you always,
William Keepin, Ph.D. in mathematical physics, doctor of humane
letters from CIIS in spirituality and social justice

S tan, I first learned of you and your work in 1991 when I was introduced to holotropic breathwork (with Igor Weisz) in Reno, Nevada. Around the same time, by chance or synchronicity, I found a copy of *Beyond the Brain* in Reno's one "new age" bookstore. Reading that book was, with no exaggeration, life changing. Brilliant, revolutionary, and powerfully insightful, your writing gave me at last a language for my experience, a map for understanding those experiences, and the confidence to study transpersonal psychology and, later, to train to facilitate the breathwork.

And there must be, quite literally, thousands of similar stories . . .

On the very first page of *Beyond the Brain,* in the Acknowledgments, you wrote: "In all the stages of [my] long quest, the professional and personal dimensions were so intimately interwoven that they have merged into an inseparable amalgam. It has been a journey of personal transformation and self-discovery as much as a process of scientific exploration of uncharted territories of the human psyche."

Those of us who have been so fortunate to study with you, and learn from you, recognize this in the generous depths of your presence, and your extraordinary breadth of knowledge, and your rare willingness, as a scientist, to be humbly and deeply changed by your direct experience.

What you have brought forth is a profound gift to humanity—the roots go deep, the branches spread steadily and reach far, all around our beautiful planet.

Thank you, with all my heart.

May this day, and every day, bring you ever more love and happiness.

Marianne Murray, Ph.D.,
faculty member at the Academy for the Love of Learning
and board member of Grof® Legacy Project, USA

One of the myriad people whose lives have been changed for the better by your life, your work, and your presence, I offer my sincerest love and gratitude for what you have brought into the world. The vastness of your vision, coupled with the immensity of energy and intelligence you have devoted to articulating it brought so much into psychiatry and psychology that is revolutionary and humane.

When I have been in your presence, what I feel is the depth of love and caring for life that you radiate to those around you. To offer so much to the world from that well of deep caring and the motivation to support others in their journey toward wholeness is a remarkable accomplishment.

May the coming days and years bring you deepening of love and satisfaction.

With much love,
Pamela Stockton, M.A., L.P.C.,
L.P.C.C., S.E.P., psychotherapist

A lthough I've only met Stan in person once and by zoom once I would like to acknowledge the invaluable contributions he has made to so many aspects of the therapeutic mental health field. A deep bow of gratitude to you both for continuing to carry on Stan's work.

And of course Happy Birthday to Stan,
Patty Nagle, M.A., LMHC, events manager
and Grof ® Breathwork facilitator

Dear Stan,

You have so generously shared your profound insights into the human psyche. You have opened the understanding that psyche precedes birth, extending across the spectrum of cultures and the evolutionary history of our planet. And you have showed us that the opening to this vastness lies within, revealed by cultivating an amplified mental process of consciousness of our experience.

You have grown psychology to a fullness by harvesting ancient wisdom in combination with psychology's twentieth-century insights to develop a scientific paradigm that supplants Cartesian materialism and sets a course for a psychology of the future built on exceptional experience.

You have taught by example, combining theory and practice, and always demonstrating your deep compassion, listening and engaging profoundly. Knowing you and learning from you has helped us understand ourselves in ways we had never imagined and given us to develop relationships that have continued to grow and deepen over the years.

In this your 90th year we celebrate you with much love and gratitude, and all best wishes for many years to come.

Elizabeth and Lenny Gibson, Ph.D.,
directors, Dreamshadow Group Inc.

Dear Stan,

You helped to change the course of my life before we even met. My dad was in a month-long workshop with you at Esalen in the mid-seventies. He spoke fondly of that experience, how you invited him to try your flotation tank, and that he admired and loved you. From that point on, he was always supportive of my efforts toward healing and self-exploration.

In the fall of 1980, I was the youngest participant in another of your month-long seminars. What an amazing, horizon-expanding experience! I am so grateful for the richness of that opportunity. When I was going through kundalini-fueled emotional process a few years later and returned to the oasis of Esalen for comfort, you held my hand unconditionally at one point in Huxley when I really needed it. Thank you.

Later on, as a gate guard doing nightshifts at Esalen, I would walk through the serene Big House in the middle of the night and marvel at the wealth of beautiful mandalas spread across the walls, drawn by your participants. Their deep emotional processing created a truly sacred atmosphere that permeated the air of Esalen.

I am very grateful for your cofounding of transpersonal psychology. You have set forth a viable and effective pathway to psychological healing and transcendence, and yet without creating a religion, but rather as an academic discipline. Such a valuable contribution. I have also been deeply inspired by your books—*Realms of the Human Unconscious, LSD Psychotherapy, Beyond the Brain, The Adventure of Self-Discovery, Way of the Psychonaut* and many others—but of all these my favorite is *The Cosmic Game*, which I consider the book of the millennium.

Thank you for all your kindness, support, and patience over the years. I wish you the good health to continue enjoying the sweet and loving fruits of your well-lived life, and am grateful you are with us now to witness the rebirth of responsible psychedelic research.

With much love and appreciation,
Renn Butler, Ph.D., author of The Archetypal Universe
and Pathways to Wholeness *and cofounder of the*
Archetypal News Network (ANN) YouTube channel

Hello Stan,

I would like to wish you wonderful birthday wishes and bountiful days. You have meant so much to me that I would like to express how you have impacted my life and work. In 2007 my oldest son who was seventeen years old died in a car crash on the way to his hockey game in the next town. Sam was everything to me. His plan was to study medicine and eventually psychiatry, asking me not to retire until we were able to work together in the practice of psychiatry. I was devastated by his death. Modern psychology and psychiatry had no help for my grief. I hit the books looking for some solution and kept running across your name. So many books are written by people with little real experience that I needed to be in your presence and experience holotropic breathwork led by you.

In my first breathwork experience I had a full BPM I, II, III, IV experience ending up on my mother's breast feeling her love for me. This experience required me to change my view about my mother and other women in my life. I also realized in that experience that Mary, the mother of Jesus, also lost a son and that I shared a deep connection with her and all parents that have lost children. Experiencing that holotropic states have tremendous healing potential, I did the training program and became a breathwork facilitator, running breathwork groups over the years. I continued my own healing, working with Ralph Metzner until he passed on.

I have had the privilege of working with people in Canada with end-of-life distress helping them to get government exemptions for legal access to psilocybin mushrooms and then working with them as you taught from your experience in Prague and then at the Maryland Psychiatric Institute when psychedelics were legal. I was also given an exemption for legal psilocybin mushroom use by the Canadian Federal Minister of Health at the time, the Honorable Patty Haidu, to further my own learning and healing. I am also part of a group of six physicians and health care practitioners from Canada, the U.S., and Jamaica that do weeklong group retreats in Jamaica where we use psilocybin mushrooms for parents who have lost a child and are stuck in their grief.

I am also privileged to be an Assistant Clinical Professor at the University of British Columbia in Canada. In my position at UBC I am able to teach medical students, family practice residents, and psychiatry residents, as well as other physicians and psychiatrists, about your model of the healing potential of holotropic states of consciousness. I am deeply grateful for your selfless giving of your knowledge and expertise so this wisdom of the ages can be passed down to future generations for the healing of anyone who desires it. My heart is warmed as I'm sure yours is every time we see someone whose pain has decreased from their work in a holotropic state. Thank you Stan from the totality of my being for your work, teaching, and generosity. I can truly say that you showed me the way out of my pain, and your teaching is showing other people the way out of their pain, toward health. Again, thank you.

*Neil Hanon, M.D., psychiatrist, teacher,
founding board member of GLT Canada*

My birthday wish for you, Stan, is that we who are part of Grof Legacy Training can keep expanding your holotropic vision by passing it on to the future forever. You and your life's work have been an inspiration to me since my first holotropic breathwork workshop in 1993. Inspire is from the Latin *inspirare* "to breathe or blow into."

One of my early mandalas was titled "breathing life into me!" Grof Breathwork not only breathed more life into me, but becoming a facilitator and holding space for those in non-ordinary states of consciousness led to a new level of inspiration. Experiences as both breather and facilitator initiated me into deeper meanings of being human in this life. Moreover, my experiences on the mat and in workshops with others was expanded by reading your work. I knew what you were teaching was true time and again from my own experiences and what I witnessed others experiencing. After my first session, I checked out *LSD Psychotherapy* from the Vancouver public library and kept reading and learning. Holotropics has held my attention for thirty years now and my fascination and involvement is only getting stronger. The aphorism "When you reach the top, you should remember to send the elevator back down for others" is the essence of legacy and resonates strongly with me. Now that the prohibition period has given way to a renaissance in psychedelic psychotherapy, I am honored to join your worldwide community of trainers to pay it forward to the next generation.

Carolyn J. Green, BHS (Physio), Ph.D.,
researcher, founding member GLT Canada

Stan,

In one capacity or another, Donna and I have worked with you for over forty years. In all that time, and in contradistinction to many teachers we have met, you never wanted from us money, sex, or power. All you wanted was that we should learn and practice transpersonal psychology. And for that we respect you as deeply as we love you. For us, the lineage to which we proudly belong is Freud, Jung, and Grof. Plus quite a bit of wonderfulness on the transpersonal side.

> May the long time sun shine on you
> All love surround you
> And the pure light within you
> Guide your way out.

Amor e Luz,
Sean O'Sullivan, M.D., Emergency Department physician and
psychedelic psychotherapist and Donna Rosenthal, B.A., certified
in holotropic breathwork, psychedelic therapist and lecturer

Sean, Stan, Francine, and Donna

Susan and Stan

Dear Stan,

May your birthday be filled with joy, and the years ahead be a source of ever expanding peace and understanding. Your courage, wisdom, and curiosity have helped me
nurture those qualities in myself, and I will be forever grateful for what has opened
as a result of following your example. My heart is warmed to think of our friendship and my soul comforted knowing your wisdom is spreading in the world. It has
been an honor and a pleasure to work with you these past years.

Much love to you,
Susan Hess Logeais, filmaker,
permaculture and regeneratve agriculture student,
founding member of Hot Flash Films PDX

For Stan Grof, on His 90th Solar Return

S tan, my first meeting with you was while I was still in utero, immersed in the sacred, enchanted womb of the first perinatal matrix, and thus there was never a time in my life when you were not already present. Your name in our household was always one used with respect and reverence, but also with intimacy and affection. My little childhood consciousness came to know you first through the many cartoon animations you would draw for me—of whales and elephants, gorillas and ducks, or a smiling and playful Mickey Mouse. You were a loving presence whenever you came into our home, and your deep voice always resonated with a warm comfort to my young ears.

Only slowly did a realization begin to dawn of your professional significance as a psychiatrist and researcher of consciousness, and about the time my teenage mind was being introduced to the concept—not yet the experience—of LSD and psychedelics, the revelation came that I already knew one of the foremost pioneers in this field. The true significance of your role finally sunk in when I was sixteen years old, and had the privilege of joining you and my dad for a visit to Albert Hofmann's home in Switzerland. That meeting catalyzed my interest in learning your work and gaining a fuller picture of the godfather figure who had been present in my earliest memories.

Learning about your work—from the early trials of LSD psychotherapy and your discovery of the perinatal matrices, to the rich transpersonal cartography of the psyche and the extraordinary correlations with archetypal astrology—was like rediscovering something I already implicitly knew. And perhaps I already did, since transpersonal and archetypal language was spoken frequently during my childhood. Yet coming to your work in young adulthood brought that implicit knowing fully into bright consciousness, and my soul was ignited to put what I was learning from you into practice: diving deep into the psyche, exploring holotropic breathwork, seeking psychospiritual and relational healing, and coming into a deeper mystical understanding of the divine cosmos and the power of the death-rebirth mystery. In my first breathwork session, I had a vision of myself as a butterfly dancing with a great whale in the ocean. It was only later that I realized you were symbolized by that whale: a powerful yet gentle presence, quietly checking in again and again throughout the session.

Narrating the audiobook of *The Way of the Psychonaut* gave me a beautiful intimacy with your work that I could not have fully anticipated: to speak each

word of your text with the purpose of articulating the essence of your intended meanings opened up new worlds of understanding. During those nine days in the recording studio, I felt as though I was living inside your thoughts, experiencing the breadth of your life's work from the inside.

And now I have the great honor to tell your life story in the form of a biography. Each of your nine decades has its own archetypal character and narrative arc, and it is my profound delight to be able to celebrate the richness of your life through this creative work.

I wish you ten thousand blessings as you enter into this tenth decade of your life. May it be filled with wonder, fulfillment, deep joy, and laughter.

Becca Tarnas, Ph.D., scholar and author

Dear Stan,

It is hard to find words that express our gratitude for your lifelong commitment and contribution to the field of psychedelic research, transpersonal psychology, and consciousness.

In 2020, my wife Kristina and I created the Psychedelic Literacy Fund and donated resources to support the translation of books about psychedelics in different languages. When we asked ourselves what could be the first book to start with, we selected one of our favorite books that you wrote, *The Way of the Psychonaut.* We wanted to honor your life and your 90th birthday. Since then, it has been a wonderful journey in which we have had the opportunity to meet wonderful people whose lives have been changed by your work.

My journey into the field of psychedelics started by reading your books when I was sixteen years old. Now, after twenty-two years, I have the opportunity to work as literary agent for you and your wife Brigitte. What a blessing! Some of your books have been translated into different languages, but many have not (yet!). Every time a publisher from around the world expresses interest in the rights for one of your books, I think of the impact it will have on all the people who will finally be able to read it.

You recently asked me, "What are you planning to do with the editions of my books in different languages that I gave you?" My answer was, "To keep an archive of all your books, translated in different languages, and make sure that your work is preserved and accessible for generations to come." Rest assured I will do my best to fulfill this promise.

You have been a beacon of light through times of darkness, and a model of influence to many for your courage, curiosity, and humility. Thank you for touching our lives so deeply. Wishing you and Brigitte infinite joy, health, and happiness.

Much love,
Jonas di Gregorio, B.A., and Kristina Soriano, M.H.A.,
advisers of the Psychedelic Literacy Fund

Acknowledgments

I am deeply grateful for everyone who supported the publication of this book for Stan's 90th birthday. It was his deepest wish to see our interview published, because it shows who he is now after sixty-five years of research of holotropic states of consciousness. His lifelong passion for the work with LSD and his deep connection and friendship with Albert Hofmann are honored and expressed in this book. He said it was the best birthday gift he ever got in his life.

Many thanks to agent Christian Schweiger and to the team at Inner Traditions for publishing this U.S. edition—Ehud Sperling, Jon Graham, Erica Robinson, Courtney Jenkins, Jeanie Levitan, Jamaica Burns Griffin, Virginia Scott Bowman, Kenleigh Manseau, Ashley Kolesnik, and Eliza Homick—and to all the friends and colleagues for your sweet birthday wishes.

I am also very grateful for our friends from Nachtschatten Verlag, with whom I created the first print of this book in the German language and Nina Seiler for the graphics, the cover design, and photo gallery; and for Renn Butler who did the initial edit of the English text.

And last but not least a big thank you to my beloved Stan—without your knowledge this book would not exist!

Brigitte Grof
Wiesbaden, 2022

About the Authors

Stanislav Grof, M.D., Ph.D., is a psychiatrist with over sixty years of experience in research of non-ordinary states of consciousness and one of the founders and chief theoreticians of transpersonal psychology. He was born in Prague, Czechoslovakia, where he also received his scientific training: an M.D. degree from the Charles University School of Medicine and a Ph.D. degree (Doctor of Philosophy in Medicine) from the Czechoslovakian Academy of Sciences. He was also granted honorary Ph.D. degrees from the University of Vermont in Burlington, Vermont; Institute of Transpersonal Psychology in Palo Alto, California; and the World Buddhist University in Bangkok, Thailand. In 2018 he received an honorary Ph.D. degree for Psychedelic Therapy and Healing Arts from the Institute of Integral Studies (CIIS) in San Francisco, California.

Dr. Grof's early research in the clinical uses of psychedelic substances was conducted at the Psychiatric Research Institute in Prague, where he was principal investigator of a program that systematically explored the heuristic and therapeutic potential of LSD and other psychedelic substances. In 1967, he received a scholarship from the Foundations Fund for Research in Psychiatry in New Haven, Connecticut, and was invited as Clinical and Research Fellow to the Johns Hopkins University and the Research Unit of Spring Grove Hospital in Baltimore, Maryland.

In 1969, Dr. Grof became Assistant Professor of Psychiatry at the Johns Hopkins University and continued his research as Chief of Psychiatric Research at the Maryland Psychiatric Research Center in Catonsville, Maryland. In 1973, he was invited as Scholar-in-Residence to the Esalen Institute in Big Sur, California, where he developed, with his late wife Christina Grof, holotropic breathwork, an innovative form of experiential psychotherapy that is now being used worldwide. Christina Grof died in 2014; her memorial website is www.christina-grof.com.

Dr. Grof is the founder of the International Transpersonal Association (ITA) and for several decades served as its president. In 1993, he received a Honorary Award from the Association for Transpersonal Psychology (ATP) for major contributions to and development of the field of transpersonal psychology, given at the occasion of the 25th Anniversary Convocation held in Asilomar, California. In 2007, he received the prestigious VISION 97 lifetime achievement award from the Foundation of Dagmar and Václav Havel in Prague, Czechoslovakia. In 2010, he received also the Thomas R. Verny Award from the Association for Pre- and Perinatal Psychology and Health

(APPPAH) for his pivotal contributions to this field. He was also invited as consultant for special effects in the Metro Goldwyn Meyer science fiction movie *Brainstorm* and 20th Century Fox science fiction movie *Millenium.*

Among Dr. Grof's publications are over 160 articles in professional journals and many books.

In August 2019 his life's work encyclopedia *The Way of the Psychonaut* was published and the documentary film about his life and work got released—*The Way of the Psychonaut: Stanislav Grof's Journey of Consciousness.*

His books have been translated into twenty-two languages: German, French, Italian, Spanish, Portuguese, Dutch, Swedish, Danish, Russian, Ukrainian, Slovenian, Romanian, Czech, Polish, Bulgarian, Hungarian, Latvian, Greek, Turkish, Korean, Japanese, and Chinese.

His website is: **StanGrof.com**

Brigitte Grof, M.A., is a Dipl. Psychologist, licensed psychotherapist, and artist with over thirty-five years of experience in holotropic breathwork and Holotropic States of Consciousness. In 1986 she was trained at the Esalen Institute in California by the Grofs and got certified in the first training groups in the U.S. and Switzerland. From the beginning of the Grof Training, she has been teaching training modules in the U.S., France, and in Germany (with Dr. Sylvester Walch) and was leading a three-year holotropic breathwork training group with Dr. Ingo Jahrsetz. Since 2004 she developed and has been teaching her own method of individual therapy combining breathing and bodywork based on holotropic principles. Currently she works in her private practice in Wiesbaden, Germany, and offers holotropic breathwork workshops and retreats.

Her artwork is inspired by her own experiences of non-ordinary states of consciousness and by shamanic art of native cultures. Her book *The True King,* a spiritual fairy tale with her narrative and illustrations, has been translated by Stanislav Grof and recently published in English.

In 2022 she received an honorary Ph.D. from Ubiquity University for her lifelong work with Transpersonal Psychology, holotropic breathwork, Holotropic States of Consciousness and art, and for co-creating the international Grof® Legacy Training together with her husband Stanislav Grof.

Her website is **BrigitteGrof.com**

Since April 2016, Stan and Brigitte Grof have been happily married; they live together in Germany and travel in the inner and outer worlds in tandem. In the last years they conducted Grof® Breathwork workshops and trainings in China, Chile, Ecuador, the U.S., Sweden, Czech Republic, France, Switzerland, Argentina, Peru, and at Esalen Institute, California. In 2017 they presented their artwork and gave talks about it at the International Transpersonal Conference in Prague.

In May 2020 they launched together their new training in working with Holotropic States of Consciousness, the international Grof® Legacy Training.

Grof® Legacy Training
www.grof-legacy-training.com

In May 2020 Stanislav Grof and his wife Brigitte Grof launched their new international Grof® Legacy Training, which is based on Stanislav Grof's research into psychedelic therapy, holotropic breathwork, transpersonal psychology, and spiritual emergencies. His work has been published in two comprehensive volumes *The Way of the Psychonaut: Encyclopedia for Inner Journeys,* television courses, lectures, interviews, and many books.

Participants in this training will develop theoretical and practical knowledge and skills that are the result of more than sixty years of research of holotropic states of consciousness—a large category of non-ordinary states that have a healing, transformative, heuristic, and evolutionary potential. Holotropic states were discovered and coined by Stanislav Grof; the term *holotropic* means literally "moving toward wholeness."

Holotropic is a new word (neologism) that is composed of two Greek words— *holos,* meaning whole and *trepo/trepein,* meaning moving toward or being attracted by something. Holotropic is related to the commonly used term *heliotropism*— the property of plants to always move in the direction of the sun. The holotropic states of consciousness that the participants will study in our training represent a common denominator for phenomena that are important in health and emotional disorders of the human psyche.

Training authorized under Grof® Legacy Training will be conducted by qualified teachers under the Grofs' supervision within various countries or regions of the world the way Stan Grof would like it to be taught. In the Grof® Legacy Training, experience and instruction in holotropic breathwork will be given under the brand name Grof® Breathwork.

Stan Grof is no longer associated with the Grof Transpersonal Training (GTT) and its brand of Holotropic Breathwork® seminars and workshops.

The trainees will learn to become:
- Sitters, facilitators, and experiencers in psychedelic sessions
- Supporters of persons in spiritual emergency
- Facilitators, breathers, and sitters in holotropic sessions (GROF® Breathwork)
- Students of transpersonal psychology
- Assistants with dying people
- Apprentices in the study of archetypal astrology for work with holotropic states of consciousness

Grof® Legacy Training will provide abundant resources for both teachers and students from Stan's sixty decades of consciousness research. These resources include books, videos, PowerPoint presentations, articles, paintings, films, audios, and telecourses for which we will have permission.

Resources will be available for
Grof® Legacy Training for teachers and students
The two volumes of *The Way of the Psychonaut* are the basic sources of the training. This two-volume encyclopedia has been specifically created to provide all the most important information for taking or guiding inner journeys (psychedelic and holotropic breathwork sessions) and in working with Spiritual Emergencies. All the chapters are provided with literature that will help teachers and students give lectures and write papers or dissertations.

The *Psychonaut* books will be accompanied by ninety minutes of the film bearing a similar name: *The Way of the Psychonaut: Stanislav Grof's Journey of Consciousness*, produced by Susan Hess Logeais.

The *Psychonaut* books are translated into many world languages (Spanish, Portuguese, German, French, Russian, Czech, Chinese). This will enable students to read these books at home and deepen all that they learn in their classes. The *Psychonaut* movie, the telecourses, and all our teaching materials have subtitles or are translated in the languages of the countries where the trainings are conducted.

Telecourses:
Psychology of the Future (Shift Network) .... 7 weeks
The Way of the Psychonaut (Shift Network) ....24 weeks
Is Archetypal Astrology the Rosetta Stone
    of the Human Psyche? (Shift Network).................8 weeks (with Rick Tarnas)
Psyche and Cosmos (Shift Network) ....16 weeks (with Rick Tarnas)

Holotropic States of Consciousness:
Technologies of Sacred (Science and Non/Duality)
1. Radical Revision of Psychology
2. Spiritual Emergency
3. Understanding Violence and Greed
4. Cosmic Game

Podcast
Tim Ferriss's Interview with Stanislav Grof (close to three hours).

Teaching videos about bodywork and music and manual for working with Holotropic States of Consciousness (by Stan and Brigitte Grof 2021)

Other than occasions where Stan and/or Brigitte Grof will teach in an individual Grof® Legacy Training program, the Grofs will not receive any profit from Grof® Legacy Training or from the trademark Grof®. Grof® Legacy Training and the brand name Grof® Breathwork for Stan and Christina Grof's technique of holotropic breathwork have been created with the goal of protecting and spreading the Grof® work in the quality Stan wishes his work to be represented. Stan and Brigitte Grof believe it belongs to the world and should be taught for the generations to come.

Works by Stanislav Grof

Grof, Stanislav. *The Adventure of Self-Discovery*. Albany: State University of New York Press, 1988.

———. *Beyond the Brain*. Albany: State University of New York Press, 1985.

———. *Beyond Death: The Gates of Consciousness*. London: Thames & Hudson, 1980.

———. *Books of the Dead: Manuals for Living and Dying*. London: Thames & Hudson, 1994.

———. *The Cosmic Game*. Albany: State University of New York Press, 1998.

———. *Healing Our Deepest Wounds*. Newcastle, Wash.: Stream of Experience Productions, 2012.

———. *LSD: Gateway to the Numinous*. Rochester, Vt.: Park Street Press, 2009. Originally published as *Realms of the Human Unconscious,* New York: Viking Press, 1975.

———. *LSD Psychotherapy*. Sarasota, Fla.: Multidisciplinary Association for Psychedelic Research, 2001.

———. *Modern Consciousness Research and the Understanding of Art*. Santa Cruz, Calif.: Multidisciplinary Association for Psychedelic Research, 2015.

———. *Psychology of the Future*. Albany: State University of New York Press, 2000.

———. "Tentative Theoretical Framework for Understanding Dynamics of LSD Psychotherapy." Preprint for the European Conference on LSD Psychotherapy, Amsterdam, Holland, 1966.

———. *The Ultimate Journey*. Ben Lomond, Calif.: Multidisciplinary Association for Psychedelic Research, 2006.

———. *Way of the Psychonaut*. 2 vols. Santa Cruz, Calif.: Multidisciplinary Association for Psychedelic Research, 2019.

———. *When the Impossible Happens*. Boulder, Colo.: Sounds True, 2006.

Grof, Stanislav, and Christina Grof, eds. *Spiritual Emergency*. New York: Jeremy P. Tarcher, 1989.

Grof, Stanislav, and Christina Grof. *Holotropic Breathwork*. Albany: State University of New York Press, 2010.

———. *The Stormy Search for the Self*. Los Angeles: Jeremy P. Tarcher, 1990.

Grof, Stanislav, and Joan Halifax. *The Human Encounter with Death*. New York: E. P. Dutton, 1977.